THE MELANCHOLY ANATOMY OF PLAGIARISM

K. R. St. Onge

UNIVERSITY
PRESS OF
AMERICA

Lanham • New York • London

Copyright © 1988 by

University Press of America,® Inc.

4720 Boston Way
Lanham, MD 20706

3 Henrietta Street
London WC2E 8LU England

All rights reserved

Printed in the United States of America

British Cataloging in Publication Information Available

ISBN 0-8191-6860-2 (pbk. : alk. paper)
ISBN 0-8191-6859-9 (alk. paper)

All University Press of America books are produced on acid-free paper which exceeds the minimum standards set by the National Historical Publications and Records Commission.

```
PN        St. Onge, K. R.,
167       1920-
S7
1988      The melancholy
          anatomy of
          plagiarism
```

$10.25   g

Table of Contents

Chapter   Page

Note to the Reader vii
Prologue   ix
   I.   PSYCHOBIOLOGY   1
  II.   LANGUAGE DEVELOPMENT   9
 III.   LANGUAGE PEDAGOGY   17
 IV.   LANGUAGE AND SCHOLARSHIP   25
   V.   ACADEMIC ETHICS   33
 VI.   ACADEMIC EQUITY AND DEBT   45
 VII.   DEFINITIONS AND CONCEPTS   51
VIII.   CHARGES   63
 IX.   COPYING PRACTICES AND EXAMPLES   71
   X.   THE BIDEN CASE   79
 XI.   DEFENSES   91
 XII.   PROOF   99
Epilogue 101
Bibliography 103
Index 105

NOTE TO THE READER

Senator Biden's problems should remind us of how demoralizing and devastating charges of plagiarism can be, of how the verdict is embedded in the charge itself, and how voracious the appetites of accusers and spectators for details of the "tragic flaw." But it is not good theater, nor a fair fight. Real people are inflicting real pain. The unhappy reality is that plagiarism, whatever else it is, is an exercise in pure pain: purposely inflicted to inhibit or punish.

The intent of this monograph is to challenge our consciences to open the debate and shift the grounds of analysis from purported offenses to the defensibility of the standards we use in protecting whatever equity is justified in someone else's syntax. That, presumably, is what the idea of plagiarism is supposed to do. Is that what it ought to do? Is that what it is doing? Is it doing what we really want it to do? These questions, largely unasked and unanswered, if launched, will sail against the prevailing traditional winds. It will be a rough passage, even without foundering before the breakwater is reached. (The metaphor needs relief.) This academic senior citizen is saddling up Rosinante for one more ride. Tilting at the plagiarism windmill seems a worthy quest. We all need something to do before the Knight comes.

How is it to be done? With no little agonizing. This monograph reviews the general ethical context of higher education from whence plagiarism is derived. The view is dispiriting. Education, higher education, all professionals, are subject to contemporary ethical re-evaluation if the current press is any index to our concerns. Having restated a nearly impossible ethical standard for the professoriate in the middle of the Chapter <u>Academic Ethics</u>, I must be bound by the ethics that I commend to others.

If I object to the needless, unjustified pain inflicted in the name of plagiarism, I cannot inflict new pain on old wounds nor newly wound the already wounded as I use the evidence essential to redirecting our concepts and values. The corpus of plagiaristic behavior is of enormous dimensions, with members and appendages running in all directions and out of sight. No matter how diligent, the most earnest student will never have anything but the tiniest fragment of the whole. How much is needed for a representative sample is only somewhat less obscure. The reader is asked to reflect. This is the start of the dialogue, not the end.

A half of a century in higher education as student, professor, administrator, a diligent reader, inveterate scribbler, and selective file keeper, these old eyes have rolled in large amounts of delight punctuated by episodes of dismay. They have seen the copywork of undergraduates, graduates, colleagues, and administrators. If there is any one of us who hasn't seen the same, one would wonder whether that rare soul occupies the same universe or is really paying attention.

The examples used in this monograph are not numerous but the analysis is based on many episodes involving most species of copying. The reader alone can judge whether the experiences are representative and the conclusions fairly derived. Meaning no hurt, only the already well ventilated instances are fully documented. Those later in time and closer to home have only such documentation necessary to the issue at hand or have omitted altogether explicit references that would link any specific individual to any specific instance.

Despite possible contrary appearances, the author's position is quite explicit. Necessary copying should be properly credited. All else should be original work of the writer. But such a standard can apply only to those with the essential literate skills. The standard is not only ethically based but psychologically sound. It is grounded in the need for all educated individuals to do their own thinking. It is good to replicate the good and the great. It is greater by far to continue the process of generating and testing ideas. Let the ideas of plagiarism face the test.

PROLOGUE

About two thousand years ago when writing was much younger, some writers became so enamored of their expository labors that they resented those who copied their works. These gentlemen, on the whole a rather eloquent group, complained bitterly and cast about for ways to inhibit the temptation to copy and especially to deter copiers from taking credit for the works of others. By more or less common consent, the originators felt themselves to have had their verbal pockets picked. So they complained of theft, larceny, and abduction. Hence, <u>plagiarism,</u> to <u>steal away</u>, or <u>kidnap</u>, or <u>abduct</u> the words of others.

Since then we have added to the moral offense of plagiarism, the legal one of infringement. It is now thought fitting to protect authors from themselves and others. Because communication consists primarily of copying (and in that respect it differs not from any other artifacts of our culture) instruction was thought necessary in licit and illicit forms of it.

Thereby, the cottage industry of plagiarism was born, with face-offs between the plagiarer and the plagiaree in bouts of plagiary. And very interesting contests they were and are, and for bystanders a lively subspecies of the entertainment industry except for certain kill-joys inclined to lament the spirited fratricides of the literate. The parable of plagiarism is a story for us all since it is a symptom complex of pedagogical, linguistic, intellectual, professional, ethical, and legal dimensions. It is also a metaphor: getting on and off the oddly run verbal carousel, for plagiarism whether real or alleged informs on us as a verbalizing, symbol-driven species.

From time to time the subject forces itself upon us. The "plagiarism" of students in essays, outlines, term papers and speeches, of faculty extractions made without credit, of charges of plagiarism in the academic arena, and cases of plagiarism alleged or actual in the academic press. Perhaps we are inured to small infractions and perhaps as well, secretly delighted to find others guilty of larger infractions. But when the finger is pointed, the ill-defined threshold of someone's sensibilities having been crossed, men's egos, ambitions and envy, outraged innocence, righteous indignation, all square off for sometimes brutal confrontations.

A significant contribution to culture, art, science, pedagogy is guaranteed to grant a modest immortality and an increment to relative wealth and status. There is sufficient motivation to keep the plagiarism industry going, the offended parties protesting, and the innocent parties objecting. Has the process changed? Has society changed in relation to concepts of plagiarism? Do we know or only think we know what we are talking about when discussing plagiarism? Is there a syndrome of plagiarism or is there just a set of human communication behaviors to which some human communicators object?

As all terms with some currency, necessarily a long history entails. All of the early classic examples of plagiarism, alleged, or real. Earlier didactic tracts intended to enlighten us on the mysteries and peculiarities of plagiarism, such as Lindey's <u>Plagiarism and Originality</u>. Later critical tracts, such as Peter Shaw's "Plagiary." Contemporary law suits. Early legal concepts of plagiarism. Standard definitions of plagiarism. Modes of plagiarism. Reflexive plagiarism, i.e., plagiarism of the already plagiarized. The psychology of plagiarism. Plagiarism of the great and of the insignificant: works or authors. Plagiarism in the arts, the sciences, music, painting, literature, research, scholarship, student or professor. Bits of plagiarism, bigger bites, through wholesale expropriation.

It is simply not possible to know the entire literature any more than it is possible to review all species of examples. There is one irreducible fact from which all might get started. We are invariably speaking about communication patterns, largely language or linguistic symbolic analogues. Hence, we can start with contemporary linguistic notions of the surface and deep structures of plagiarism. Either there are rules and laws pertaining to the term or the term itself is a useless, even pernicious, entity. Any term potentially applicable to the entirety of communication must be suspect on the fact of it and disciplined to differentiate validly based on the enormously diverse contexts in which communication is conducted, in purpose, in value, in originality, and in the kind of labor communication entails.

Prologues are used to put readers on course but must arise from the retrospective of having run it. What is surprising in this heterodoxical era is the extreme lack of intellectual rigor and impunity accorded plagiarism. What if it is the last sacred cow of scholarship and pedagogy kept in the pasture of ethics as a remnant of values past, and possibly all that remains of academic ethics? We are obliged to understand the temptation to copy on the part of those for whom written expression hovers between the arduous and the impossible. As we are obliged to provide realistic and practical guidance to all who aspire to see in print their words or somebody's words associated with their efforts.

This monograph is a kind of owner's manual to the innate symbolic processors within us all and a handbook on how to avoid plagiarism, how to commit it with minimal risks of detection, how to handle charges of plagiarism, guilty or not, when to charge others with plagiarism, and how to select and combine optimum defenses for any innocents who may stumble into plagiarism's many traps. The <u>Compleat Plagiary</u> starts with the raw materials of communication and ends with examples, demonstrations, and proof. Take hope all who enter here.

I

THE PSYCHOBIOLOGY OF PLAGIARISM

It is a fair question to ask what educated people think plagiarism is before the grind of line-by-line, case-by-case, and definition-by-definition analysis deadens the sensibilities. The analysis of plagiarism can start too far back as well as far too deep. It may not even be the almost exclusive concern of the well educated. The behavior of people who "ought to know" is probably the best inductive route to their understandings. Thereafter, the road gets long and steep as the progression of plagiarism concepts is followed through the eyes, and sometimes minds, of scholars and experts.

Petty Verbal Larceny

William Childress, essayist for the <u>St. Louis Post-Dispatch</u>, remembered that he was accused of plagiarism at the age of seven. He wrote a poem for his teacher, a quatrain of four lines. The second line was "Like diamonds in the sky. . . ." When reminded decades later, she responded, "'Like diamonds in the sky' came from 'Twinkle, Twinkle Little Star.' You embarrassed me, Willy." Mr. Childress has had about forty-five years to reflect on his offense. (Actually, I recall the line as "Like <u>a</u> diamond in the sky." Childress could have claimed a poetic adaptation to his first line.) But age seven is much too early for such polemics. What is disturbing is that a school teacher forty-five years ago should have lodged such a lethal pedagogical complaint against one so young and on such insubstantial grounds. Would the child have been safe with quotation marks? Would the work of the incipient poet have been held in lesser esteem? And what of the traumatized Mr. Childress who confronts, although only his imagination, his teacher of long ago with a reproach in hindsight? He writes, "I embarrassed <u>you</u>, Miss Blank? I didn't even know what plagiarism was. I thought it was okay to borrow from another poem." And Mr. Childress still doesn't know what plagiarism is. Yet when we recall how editorial criticism has withered us, our spirits must be with him. But this does little to settle the pedagogy of plagiarism. The example is trivial but the charge was brutal. One thing has been learned. There is no necessary correspondence between the alleged offense and the punishment that may ensue.

A popular handbook on English composition has an appendix titled, <u>Avoiding Plagiarism</u>. It may be assumed that there is no more authoritative source. It says, "Even a phrase from a poem, such as 'miles to go before I sleep' is literature--not folk

1

literature--and requires acknowledgement" [emphasis added]. What kind of a title did Robert Frost have to such a phrase? How many people said the identical phrase before he ever inserted it into his famous poem? If I now write "miles to go before I eat," does Frost get part credit, i.e., five sixths? The line by itself is most prosaic. As it stands, it certainly is not original. It is folk speech for which Robert Frost didn't give credit. Lindey says, "A dozen paragraphs taken from a long book may be fair use; four lines from a six-line poem may be an infringement." But six words from "Stopping by Woods on a Snowy Evening" is plagiarism? Or may set off charges? The low end of plagiarism is almost without bottom. Is there more to learn in semi-trivial cases?

Suppose I were to write and publish this sentence: "Through carelessness, I have lost all track of time and now time is losing, rapidly, all track of me," and the quotation marks signify that the words are from the mouth of an historical character set in a piece of fiction. Then a critical reader of rich literary background remembers another piece of fiction and another historical character saying, "I wasted time and now doth time waste me." Is the first quote a poor paraphrase of the second? The quotes obviously share a common idea. Have I plagiarized an idea in the course of the paraphrases? Is the first quote an original sentence embodying a common idea? Quite possibly. Are the two quotes absolutely independent? Not likely. What is the real context?

The first quote is from Gore Vidal's latest novel, Empire. The second is from Shakespeare's Richard the 2nd. A profound student of literature with nothing better to do could reduce Vidal's novel to its derivative intellectual roots, conclude rightly or wrongly that Vidal had nothing significant to say or nothing new to say. And then wonder where Shakespeare got the idea. The idea that ideas can be plagiarized is not a good idea. It leads inevitably to such questions as who first thought the idea; who said it first, wrote it first, best expressed it, and published first, in what must be an infinite regression into the past. Plots, motifs, ideas, themes, and titles do not have the privilege of copyright with good reason. Yet no one has suggested that ideas and "apt phrases" be excluded from the grounds of plagiarism.

An instance was presented in a column by Bob Greene, St. Louis Post-Dispatch, October 24, 1984, headed, "Why A Person Steals Words." The article starts, "The journalistic and literary sin [sic] that has always puzzled me the most is plagiarism." Mr. Greene found himself plagiarized through an alert third party who identified the plagiarizer. Mr. Greene assured the third party that he was not inclined to take any action against the plagiarizer, but did want to talk to the person to better understand his motivation. The plagiarizer had been having job and personal problems. In summary, here is his verbatim motivation as explained to Mr. Greene:

> I am 50 years old. I don't have any legitimate excuse for what I did. I've been trying so hard to get recognized and be accepted in my job and I haven't been doing that well. I thought that people would see it (the article) and that they would think well of me. I had intended to write something of my own. But then I saw your story and I liked it, and for some reason, I just changed a few things and put my name on top of it. I knew I was doing wrong, but I did it anyway. I truthfully don't think of myself as a generally dishonest person.

It turns out that the materials plagiarized in the above instance had originally appeared as authored by Mr. Greene in a national magazine. The plagiarizer had taken the article in its entirety, made strategic alterations, put his name on it, and it was republished under the name of the pseudo-author, which makes it something more than petty verbal larceny.

Emotional instability, questionable expositional skills, and temptation is the complex that lurks in the background of reported plagiarisms. Writing is extremely hard work. Writing well enough to be published is unlikely on the face of it. Old trunks are full of unpublished manuscripts. The published is a small to negligible fraction of what is written. Mr. Green's plagiarizer sounds exactly like all of us who plan to write something, someday soon. We can sympathize with the procrastination. We do not know whether this procrastinator turned plagiarizer actually had strong enough expositional skills to be published on his own merits. His ethics were weak. But if he had ordinary prudence, would he have taken an article from a national publication and submitted it as his own to a local newspaper? It is probably more than a case of typical midlife crisis.

Then there is this special notice in the <u>Chronicle of Higher Education</u>, June 10, 1987:

> NOTICE: Several readers of <u>The Chronicle</u> have called our attention to the fact that the May 20 "Point of View" article by Leo Ochrymowycz closely resembled--and, in places, duplicated word for word--an essay by Carter A. Daniel that appeared on our "Point of View" page of May 7, 1979. In response to a query from the editors of <u>The Chronicle</u>, Mr. Ochrymowycz acknowledged that the work was not original with him, that he had come across it in the form of an unsigned copy that circulated on his campus, and that he regretted that he had used

the piece as if it were his own. He has agreed to return the payment he received from The Chronicle. --The Editor

One can only imagine the discussions going on at Professor Ochrymowycz's campus and among the editorial staff of The Chronicle on learning that it was plagiarizing itself. By an editorial lapse, it had misled its readers into thinking they were reading an original article as the copier/paraphraser had similarly misled The Chronicle. The readers got no apology. The Chronicle got its money back. The species of copying went unlabeled, Ochrymowycz went unlibeled, and the student of plagiarism went unenlightened as to context. [Please see Chapter IX for excerpt.]

The Sprawling Syndrome

The cliche very probably only rarely applies, but plagiarism actually does span the gamut from the "sublime to the ridiculous." The ridiculous and trivial provide, as we have seen, explicit examples. The other extreme, the grand verbal larceny of the great, appears even less explicable.

The syndrome of plagiarism appears to include a large diversity of signs and symptoms. In the chain of causation, are the roots of plagiarism at the front end or back? Does the plagiarist have an eye on the gratifying consequences of successful fraudulent authorship or on the immediate travails of engaging in the struggle to produce an original work? Certainly, lack of talent and/or intellectual drive, lack of confidence, chronic or periodic, must be included in the list of motivations that lead to plagiarizing.

Both Alexander Lindey and Peter Shaw try to get into the minds of the plagiarizer. Lindey attributed plagiarism to the inducement of money, admiration, glory, ignorance, and kleptomania which he described and rightly considered as a psychopathology. Shaw develops the "kleptomania" theory stating, "The plagiarist resembles the kleptomaniac both in his evident wish to be detected and in the circumstance that what is stolen may not be needed." Lindey concludes that the plagiarist "is careful not to get caught," while Shaw in his analysis of literary plagiarism finds many examples of plagiarists who seemingly leave careless clues as to the original sources. Both experts cannot be correct but each may be partially right.

The kleptomania idea itself as advanced by both Lindey and Shaw permits a modest instructive extension of use or theft of ideas as a species of plagiarism. At the same time it raises the question of what is achieved by pursuit of idea source. Lindey compared plagiarism with kleptomania (1952). He did not prior source the idea. Peter Shaw (1982) developed the idea of plagiarism as kleptomania. He did not prior source the idea. Both experts were writing in the context of plagiarism. In this chapter (below), I have shifted plagiarism as kleptomania to plagiarism as a species of multiple verbal personality. I know of no prior source for the idea. It is profoundly unlikely that it is an original idea and only slightly less unlikely that no one has developed the idea somewhere in print and would therefore have a prior claim to the idea and/or the publishing of it.

Somewhere in the extensive literature of multiple personality it is quite possible that some writer raised the issue of plagiarism and it is also possible that some master plagiarizer is hidden among the many facets of a multiple personality syndrome. Should the sincere students of such issues address the issues directly or pursue root ideas the way etymologists peruse word roots--into the mists of the past? Should Lindey and Shaw have interrupted their tasks in favor of the historiography of ideas? And who owes what to whom in the arena of ideas?

Grand Verbal Larceny

The great plagiarizers have been at work in the verbal vineyards since the day they took root. Being both famous and linguistically supercompetent, why would they plagiarize? An increment of added fame and the economy of effort of verbal theft hardly seem sufficient inducements. In some cases perhaps. But certainly not in so many. This writer is inclined to think that both Shaw and Lindey by electing kleptomania are resorting to the wrong analogy. The problem more plausibly is linguistic for most, not ethical. The great, near great, and supergreat plagiarizers have one non-common denominator. They have in varying degrees prodigious linguistic systems. How do these systems work? Our knowledge of the central nervous system indicates that there is a collection of rather explicit linguistic powers, served by neurological subsystems that interact and have degrees of mutual autonomy as well as mutual dependencies. A few of the essentials are treated more fully in the next chapter as requisite to understanding plagiarism in its general aspects. Neither Lindey nor Shaw found "unconscious" plagiarism especially convincing. And neither does this writer. But there is a neurological parallel.

The literature of psychopathology is now rather rich with cases of multiple personality. How are they to be explained? One line of investigation is exploration of the psyche and its traumas. Another is to look at the compartmentalizing of the central nervous system. The brain is a collection of regimes, local systems of storage and control. There is a subsystem for the retrieval of words, for the initiation of syntax, for the mediation of anger, for the arousal of long term memory, etc. Indeed, the brain is a system of systems. The interconnections vary from person to person. There is ample neurological room for personality divergence. Even the most normal, given the right circumstances, may take on Jekyll and Hyde behaviors. The network that holds the system together, presumably, is what gives us the sensation of having a coherent personality. However, there is no neurological reason why complete psychic entities cannot evolve in the same skull. Insufficient or absent communication between the regimes would not allow the individual to adjudicate the contesting facets. The facets would live separate lives until the person's external behaviors were observed to be irrational or inexplicable, if actually ever externalized. Hence, our common fantasies live.

If entire, discrete psyches can inhabit the same nervous system, discrete linguistic psyches must be not only equally possible, but equally probable. Consider the legions of entities that crowded the mind of Shakespeare. Or Keat's lament that he might "cease to be before my pen has gleaned my teaming brain." The enormous palaces of verbal memory of Proust, Joyce, etc. Brain damaged autistic children often have prodigious replicative abilities in music, graphic skills, and in language the echolalia of total verbal recall. Mozart could hear an extensive musical composition and write out the total score flawlessly from memory on one hearing.

The verbal/linguistic skills of the genius level can admit direct entry of substantial verbal totalities unobtrusively registered in a local regime of long-term memory. To be tapped when circumstances dictate. To be tapped as an original source. Fully assimilated, entered, verbatim or edited, it will pour out so swiftly and surely that the reconception is greeted as composition de nuovo, both new and indigenous, even though an obvious extraction from another source. It does not have to involve either self-delusion or explanation of "unconscious" memory. All it needs is to be a separate regime as multiple personalities are separate regimes. Indeed, the multiple personalities themselves are, in large part, multiple linguistic personalities.

Senator Biden's alleged plagiarism will not place him among the great plagiarizers but he is among those who quickly assimilate the personas in the syntax of others. Once in the groove the syntax runs its course, conceivably, with little or no source awareness. In the context of Biden's paraphrases, William Buckley recently reported an exemplary 1951 instance in which the newly inaugurated president of Cornell, Dean Malott, faced dismissal for plagiarism because his inaugural address contained a few hundred words from a quite obscure source. As reported by Buckley, <u>St. Louis Post Dispatch</u>, September 29, 1987, the story was told to him by the late veteran actor, Adolphe Menjou, and a quick summary is as follows. Dean Malott invited the Cornell Board of Trustees to his study, pointed to a wall of books he had claimed to have read and asked the Board Chairman to pick one and read from it. The oral reading was hardly underway when Malott stopped the chairman and proceeded to recite verbatim some of the paragraphs that followed. Malott is then quoted as saying, "You see my problem gentlemen. I have a photographic memory and I simply cannot recall with confidence whether what I am writing is or isn't original." Malott was not dismissed. Some verbal memories are as prodigious as generalized source recall is evanescent. It is the text that entrances and the context peripherals erode quickly with time.

This is not an apology for the great plagiarizers, only an explanation. The circumstances of each instance of excessive "borrowing" would determine some of the realities of the "offense." Not all great plagiarizers could claim neurology as a shield. Some were undoubtedly malicious, indifferent, jealous, envious, dishonest, etc.; that is, subject to the same flaws and foibles typical of our human species. There is much talk of God-given talents, but not much of God-given stupidity. There is enough room in plagiarism for both.

The Major Motifs of Plagiarism

Our verbal jewels are our symbolic treasures. Only ethics and law inhibit the principle of economy of effort. Theft and deception is indigenous to the animal kingdom. We need think only of the colossal effort we humans spend to avoid the "no-work-no-eat" ethic. What kind of work is the work of language? It is a powerful stimulator and inhibitor of human behavior. Language becomes itself a commodity. Trademarks, logos, mottos, slogans, motifs, apt phrases, the mot juste, aphorisms, have values as symbolic currency. Even the rather feeble "almighty" dollar is merely a paper promissory note, a symbol that stands for some relative temporary value.

"We hold these truths to be self-evident" that some phrases, sentences, paragraphs are considered immortal. We pay for the original, powerful, and sometimes valid. Most symbolic currency is quickly depreciated. We do not pay for cliches, platitudes, copy work, redundancies, unless they take on new forms or meanings to capture our rather short attention and interest spans. But language is a great font of new forms, perhaps the very greatest.

What is needed to understand plagiarism are the biologies of language and deception, the pedagogies of language and ethics, the evolution of the ideas of plagiarism, and how the definitions of the concept have worked out in practice. Then plagiarism can be placed in the full context of human behavior. Deception and mimicry have been carried to the level of fine arts in the biological enterprises from the virus to such sanctioned frauds as acting, ghost writing, fiction as fact and fact as fiction, slight-of-hand, and magic in all of its forms. In short, much that entertains and delights us. Why does the plagiarist offend us? If an offense there be, is it because the plagiarist has committed some form of original sin? And is plagiarism to be a recurring, permanent feature of the communication landscape? Very likely! The psychobiology of plagiarism requires understanding of the major motifs of communication itself, ethics, law, deception, and the debts owed to the scholarly findings that are valid, significant, and original.

II

LANGUAGE DEVELOPMENT

Is it necessary to go to the roots of language development to understand plagiarism? It is if plagiarism is inherent in the language process itself. There is a kind of forced choice that suggests itself at this point. The explanation is in either language development or language pedagogy or perhaps in the interactions of the two. Historical and contemporary explanations simply are not persuasive.

Basic "explanations" need not be numerous. Plagiarism could be a special case of the rationalization process so common in our mental maneuvers. A few options that any basic analysis might examine are the possibilities of plagiarism being a pathology of the thinking process, a problem that starts at borders of thought and inner language, or that plagiarism in writing results from some kind of contagion brought on by the inevitable contacts with oral plagiarism which is part of the developmental process. Or does plagiarism occupy the periphery of language acquisition as a part of the family of purposes that language serves?

The evidence thus far is that the educated and the bright are mystified by plagiarism but have done little to penetrate the mystery and are rather content, even confident, of their notions about it. Therefore, in much reduced form and largely by way of reminder, a profile of language development follows and the subject of plagiarism is briefly deferred.

Because human symbolic processing represents the apex of biological evolution, the full complexity of it will elude our understandings for a least a few decades. Its very complexity explains in part the multitude of modes of analysis of language in all of its aspects. The <u>development</u> of language is at least one order of difficulty beyond the understanding of language as a cultural artifact. But since all other language "experts" persist in their brave efforts, there is no reason not to re-address the issue in this document.

Most texts on language development remind the readers of the purposes of language, which may be treated currently as the study of pragmatics,i.e., namely, what are we trying to accomplish with our utterances and statements. To say that language "communicates" is both redundant and circular. Basically, what is the purpose of language? <u>It is the process by which humans develop a model of their universe in their heads.</u> The concurrent purpose is that the model allows manipulating that universe symbolically. The result, for good or ill, is that the local environment can be modified to suit the organism. Which, of course, we humans do in multitudinous, often drastic, ways. It is absolutely essential that the model be as valid as possible.

The Universe in Our Heads

The material universe, itself, can be considered a complex symbolic code to be deciphered. Most of the entire intellectual enterprise consists of differentiating the real from the apparent in a universe of devastating complexity. Even though the symbolic code of language is a manifestation of the universe itself, the code and its extensions, mathematics, for example, have made spectacular advances in separating the real from the apparent as the organism contemplates itself in its environment. The inner codes of biology are being deciphered. The invented codes of mathematics and computer science have placed human kind on the threshold of artificial intelligence. Our invented codes trace their lineage directly to the basic code of language.

Why do we need a model and how good is it? The universe is often dangerously variable and unpredictable. It is also inherently deceptive. It doesn't necessarily mean to be mean. It is its nature. Life develops (we should say "life as we know it") in very sheltered enclaves. The biological universe is largely restricted to 100 to 0 centigrade. Most of the universe is extremely cold, dotted with superhot bodies we call stars. The earth itself is extremely hot except for its outer surfaces. The atmosphere shields the biological world from ultraviolet radiation, so-called hard radiation, excessive electrical charges, and noxious gases such as methane. The earth is close enough to the sun for adequate warmth of most of its surface, but far enough away to avoid the fate of its sister planet Venus with surface temperatures reported as 800 Fahrenheit, some 600 degrees above water's boiling point. Sufficiently sheltered, humans can survive at minus 80 Fahrenheit and above 140 but both are life threatening. Our cosmological locale is sheltered and we shelter ourselves. Many forces are at work on the planet we inhabit, molecular, atomic, electronic, photonic, chemical, gravitational, each a variable that can take on either normative or extreme values. An earthquake is an example of an extreme value. For life to survive, sensors and memories were devised by evolving organisms. The variable complexities of the universe required decoding even though the data provided by sensors was incomplete.

It would take the best of theoretical neurobiologists to explain why the animal kingdom is so variable in its sensory retrieval systems. Even more theoretical is why some kinds of energy spectra, most of profound importance biologically, evolved no specific sensors whatever such as electricity, magnetism, radio, atomic radiation, and air pressure, are examples. And why some sensors cut off at higher and lower ends of their spectra. We don't need parapsychologists telling us there are things out there beyond our senses.

Sources, Signals and Symbols

Which is to say that many things were transpiring in our universe out of reach of our sensors. It was the device of language that would ultimately compensate us for the missing data. But we did have light, sound, touch, temperature, equilibrium, and motion senses. Despite their somewhat limited ranges, there was a wealth of data to be processed. Out of that wealth evolved our discrete signal detectors. In the realm of sound, detectors emerged that could isolate specific signals from background sounds. That was actually where language started. We now refer to those linguistic signals as speech sounds or phonemes. After detectors, signal synthesizers followed. The process is now called speech sound acquisition, that in turn means the development of a code inscribed in long term memory. And a necessary precursor to replicating the signals. It is convenient and sometimes instructive to consider language as consisting of elements, processes, powers, and purposes that have interlocking and interacting consequences. The full spectrum of sequencing starts with <u>detection,</u> continues with <u>acquisition</u>, and <u>replication</u> and terminates with a special kind of output, language <u>formulation,</u> the invention and production of syntax.

The elements are <u>voice,</u> <u>signals,</u> and <u>symbols</u>. The voice, inflected or uninflected, operates as a carrier of signals. The signals of all languages are phonemes, minimal sounds or sound complexes that act as specific signals in a language, namely the consonants, vowels, and other speech sounds of the language. The symbols are words or word components such as word roots, prefixes and suffixes, those signals or aggregation of signals that take on symbolic values.

Note that the transition from signal to symbol was a quick elision. It should not be. A signal serves to command attention. A symbol serves to represent some meaning. All of the English phonemes are meaningless in their phonetic function. All symbols in their symbolic function have meanings from explicit to cryptic. The distinction is more than academic because it is complicated by a basic signal-to-symbol reality. Both are slippery characters. Signals easily become symbols by taking on meanings. Symbols easily become signals by losing meaning. Four-letter profanities, for example, lose symbolic value by over-application. As do other four-letter words such as love, hate, soul, rock, etc. Part of the genius of language is the extraordinary plasticity of signals and symbols. We humans can make them serve at our will. Or to our detriment.

Developmental Powers

The powers that move the developing organism in the direction of language competence consist of signal detection: auditory, graphic, kinetic, tactile. The acquisition powers are the phases of retention of signals and symbols by processes that escort both from short term attention to long term memory. The replicative powers consist of reproducing signals and symbols by echolalia (imitation) as needed. Echolalia is a remarkable power also having many forms and covering the entire language composite of signals, symbols, and syntax. Usually the term is used to indicate the immediate ability to reproduce what has been said by another, in word, phrase or sentence. Or even larger units.

But it is the formulative powers observed in development that are most indicative of the developmental process; powers such as babbling and jargon in sound play and vocalizing. Neologizing is the universal power to invent symbols inherent in very young, normal children that is sometimes called nonsense word play. Another not fully understood power is idioglossia, the private language usually of twins but sometimes of siblings close in age. Idioglossias have their own vocabulary and syntax quite apart from the general language into which the idioglossias have emerged. Often the idioglossic twins are bilingual--communicating in the language of the environment and in their idioglossia as circumstances dictate.

Even less understood is inner speech, that private internal dialogue which we sense as thinking, silently talking to ourselves, deliberating inside with conscious tacit verbalizing. Practically no formal attention has been directed by scholars to this leap to a private channel made, of course, very early by the child. It is an important developmental transition. To the infant/child what occurs verbally occurs orally. Whatever language encoding transpires inspires utterance automatically. To think it is to say it, if indeed thinking at those levels consists of anything more than simple associations. The context arouses, the dog is seen, the child says "doggy." However, the pragmatics of discourse cannot stay in that mode. As a practical matter we cannot talk all at once all of the time, despite some TV talk programs that might suggest otherwise. Obviously more important, the pragmatics of strategy intervene. The very young child learns that all statements, utterances, or even single words are not equally welcome. Soon the child is admonished for saying things patently true and patently false. The internalizing process starts, and in the presence of such arbitrary values, thought, ego, and sometimes wisdom join the communicative process. The private internal discourse, when it starts, can also be considered a species of tacit deception.

The Language Elements

It is apparent that normal children have prodigious powers of language invention. It is a moot question as to whether the powers of language acquisition are any less prodigious. It is necessary to review the elements that are mobilized to the linguistic purposes. Phonemes are those acoustic signals that usually sequence into symbols. In English there are thirty-five to forty different signaling units that we rather clumsily equate with the English alphabet. The sound system of English has its own distinct phonology that would be an acoustic reality had writing (phonetic or not) not intervened. Thirty to forty discrete sound elements is not a large number. But those elements appear in millions of unique contexts, the familiar contexts we would call words. The unfamiliar are nonsense symbols until they take on meanings. Using the usual rules of English phonological patterns, how many words have we generated? About a million. How many words could we generate, single syllable? Billions! Multiple syllable words--megabillions! The signal system of English for all practical human communication purposes has no limit.

Comparatively, the signal system of English is for all of its size quite small in comparison to the symbol system. The normal, mature adult has a vocabulary of about 15,000 words, the alphabet of the symbolic system. There are many ways to quantify vocabulary, but no matter which method is applied, the sheer number of units that we can retrieve instantly on command still frustrates the best efforts of our supercomputers. When we can tell a computer, "I am thinking of a four-footed mammal, weighing about 800 pounds, native to Africa, with a striped hide," and the computer says, "zebra," then the computer will have a retrieval system comparable to human powers. Except that it must be able to handle 15,000 elements. Even if it does, it can then make only a start on syntax.

The power of syntax is closely approximated by factorial mathematics. The permutations of word order of a three-word sentence is six, a four-word sentence, twenty-four, and an eight-word sentence, 40,320. A sixteen word sentence is not a long sentence. As we double the eight-word sentence to sixteen, the permutations are 22 trillion, 922 billion, 789 million, 888 thousand. Yet we decode and encode sixteen-word sentences, almost flawlessly, and at will placing each element in semantically useful syntactical order. The innate syntax device in all normal brains does this for us drawing upon the symbolic mental library of thousands of symbolic units.

Syntax is the core of language. From the word order of a simple phrase to the page-long academic, scholarly sentence/paragraph, our normative vocabulary can generate syntactical sequences in such infinite variety that one individual would have to outlive the universe itself to utter half of the permissible statements potentially possible. Quite aside from the issue of validity and significance, practically all of the utterances would be original if at all syntactic and/or grammatical.

Symbols represent the alphabet of syntax. The rules of word order appear to us to be arbitrary as are the sounds and words themselves. Only the word order of syntax keeps us from a terrible guessing game of what statements mean. Statements are frequently ambiguous enough without flawed syntax or its aesthetic relative, grammar. We need only think of random word retrieval and random word sequences to watch the symbolic system, otherwise so efficient, become semantically hopeless.

The jury is still out on whether chimps or other non-human primates have syntactical skills. If they have any, thus far the skill level is left so far behind normal human capacities that chimps are not yet ready to talk about the time of day. This is not in any measure a belittling of the actual intelligence of our fellow creatures. Animals use objects as tools. They will shape objects to function as tools, or find other objects more suitable to accomplish tasks. How do we humans differ from other animals in our tool-making capacities? Man alone uses tools to make tools to make tools, ad infinitum. This also appears to be the reality with language. Man alone uses symbols to make symbols, to make symbols, to make symbols. It is in the reflexive nature of increasing refinements that language powers our understandings and wherein being human starts.

The Innate Supersystem

It is clear that the language processing capacity of the human CNS is actually a massive super computer for storage, retrieval, and manipulation of symbols, a multisystem to decode multiple variances for which a quarter trillion nerve cells are allocated. Any device that solicits discrete elements out of a repertoire of thousands and guided by internal, unconscious rules can, instantly (usually), put a dozen different word classes into infinite syntactical permutations is simply a statistical marvel. The device at once commands the thirty-five to forty unit alphabet of phonology, the 15,000 word vocabulary and the innumerable syntactical options, monitors itself as it does it, and then makes a statement, wise, foolish, simple, complicated, valid, erroneous as it desires. All of those who want an example of a great wish fulfillment machine have it in our normal language processor. We are spared the statistical labors that would be quite beyond us, in any case. We do our feeble best with grammar, but grammar is pedagogy. Normal speech/language acquisition has no pedagogy except the ad hoc variety as in retrospect we try to study and explain how language develops and functions.

The neonate, infant, and very young child are not taught speech/language. The normal immature, developing human organism is more than ready for language. At birth, the infant differentiates voice pitches, responds to speech sound contrasts, and shortly will demonstrate differentiated vocal production. Nurturers, usually mothers, conduct the initial communicative rituals that quickly become dialogues, verbally one-sided at first, but sometimes as early as six months, and certainly by twelve to fifteen months, the dialogue is no longer one-sided. At about fifteen to eighteen months the dialogue is no longer monosyllabic on the infant's side. Syntax starts; two word utterances, i.e., **daddy go**, **mommy go**, known in the trade as pivots.

The presumably immature organism learns simultaneously the phonology, the vocabulary, the syntax, and the purposive use of language. It really cannot be reasonably argued that the infant/child is linguistically immature. The eighteen months that separate the one and one-half year old from the three year old is the epoch of maximum linguistic gains, i.e., vocabulary progresses from a few words to one and one-half thousand or more, syntax from two-word phrases to both complex and compound sentences, and the sound system of the language is complete except for some of the most complex phonemes. All without pedagogy. Embedded in biological and developmental immaturity is a supermature system for language.

There is but one explanation for this precocious performance of the otherwise obviously immature little human. Language development is innate. The specific language (or languages in the case of bilingualism) is there to be internalized. The nervous system dictates only that there be rules governing the deployment of respective elements so that the problems of decoding and encoding have guidance parameters to avoid random hunts for meanings.

The evidence for the innateness of normative language development is overwhelming. All normal infants speed through acquisition and follow sufficiently consistent patterns as they do it. It cannot be stressed too emphatically that during the primary acquisition period, eighteen to thirty-six months, the very young child is learning some six more or less discrete, yet interacting, symbolic elements: the sound system, vocabulary, word forms (such as plurals, tenses, declension), word order (syntax), sentence extension, and use of all in proper contexts, that is, making use of utterance to emerging purposes that language serves. Language is synthesized from the nurturers' infantolect, the reduced, yet quite varied, immediate, here-and-now dialogue that practically all adults intuitively use with infants and children.

The very power of language acquisition in humans is what sets mankind apart from other highly evolved species. No other species has anything akin to language. Mankind has invented thousands of them. Yet language is the start, as well as the fruition, of symbolic manipulation. It was extensible into collateral codes, such as mathematics, symbolic logic, even logic itself, and segmented communication into its basic manifestations--listening, speaking, reading and writing. It should be credited with the formal discovery of thinking. All to what purpose?

It is difficult to think of a purpose that language serves in adulthood that does not occur in the language development of a child. Sometimes the intentions of the child in communicative modes are quite obvious, at other times we can make only inferences. But is not this true also of adults? The formal study of the purposes of speech antedates even Aristotle. Classic rhetoricians rather thoroughly worked over the field. Present day scholars tend to keep rediscovering the theme of purpose in human communication. The obvious ones are to inform, persuade, actuate, inspire, interest, stimulate, ventilate, celebrate, ritualize, condemn, imprecate, inhibit, role play, console, dissemble, and deceive. In no particular order. We are now so sophisticated we can reduce the basic purposes to two: inform and disinform. With a few collateral species needing no special attention, it is left to language pedagogy to analyze and place values on communicative purposes.

Children do all of these, as do adults. Language is the tool of tools for humans. From the grand array of purposes it can serve, it is the ultimate tool. The study of language development, the failures of language development, and all pathologies of language and their remediation must appreciate adequately the full implications of the stupendous complexities and implications of this most uncommon subject. By language formulation we devise and bequeath new hypotheses and ideas to better model our intricate and sometimes treacherous universe.

III

LANGUAGE PEDAGOGY

In the vast arrays of animal behaviors, mimicry is a fine art. The mocking bird plagiarizes the calls of any one of its peers and has been known to tease human whistlers. Theft is also a common feature of animal behaviors, as has been noted. Whatever plagiarism is, it is a learned behavior that represents a response related to innate powers of language as modified by experience in language training. Language pedagogy, in effect, is primarily an effort, and a very great one, to exploit the innate oral language powers to establish the largely non-innate lexical skills of reading and writing, and its symbolic derivative, arithmetic.

Pedagogy of the Non-Innate

It should not be forgotten that the sheer complexity of walking, talking, running is so great that if left to voluntary, learned processes, such actions would be acquired so laboriously as to be developmentally useless. Walking, talking, running, climbing, swimming are usually innate throughout the animal kingdom. However, we are taking liberties with language when we say that a child has <u>learned</u> to walk. The healthy, normal child walks when ready, some earlier, some later. The fact that there is a range of innateness should not surprise us. Most neonates are innate swimmers then apparently lose the innateness and must subsequently be taught, or self-taught, to swim with some safety. For the non-innate potential, essential skills, we have developed rather elaborate pedagogies. The most elaborate by far is the pedagogy of the 3 R's.

One thing that our vast primary educational system has demonstrated beyond cavil is that reading, writing and arithmetic are for ninety-plus percent of humanity essentially non-innate. There is, of course, additional evidence to that effect. Not that aural/oral language processing does not have a pedagogy in the form of speech improvement, grammar, style and vocabulary, but that pedagogy also is rooted in the written word even if not 100 percent dependent upon it. For all practical purposes, language pedagogy is primarily that of the written word and its special off-shoot arithmetic. The innate language powers are mobilized for the awkward leap to literacy.

The contrasts between the innate and the learned should not be considered two absolute polarities. We do not know and probably never will know exactly when the mutation occurred that so strongly favored symbolic processing and syntax. Nor should it be concluded that the process has ceased. The periodic occurrences of music, mathematics, graphic arts, chess, linguist, etc. prodigies is clear evidence that a high component of innateness infuses all human potential. In some it is a "splinter skill;" in others, the innate potential is sufficiently plastic to be put to the work that the genius finds stimulating. The insect world is characterized by "wired in" immutably programmed behaviors. The animal world is characterized by creatures responsive to conditioning. The much studied "conditioned response" wherein a signal unrelated to the original stimulus becomes an "adequate" stimulus may be considered the first step on the way to symbolism since the substitute stimulus "stands for" the original.

Animals teach their young survival tactics, one of which is the use of deception and another theft, two skills that take their places in the array of behaviors that contribute to a competitive edge. Oral language obviously bestowed an enormous advantage to the earliest hominid even if of limited symbolic processing capacities. As with any other tool, it was applicable to any purposes the creature could conceive. It is no accident that language pedagogy took up the language of deception simultaneously with the language of exposition. The Sophists of ancient Greece troubled the more principled speakers of the time. The great tool of language was a power that loaned itself to the purposes of all who developed it, whatever those purposes.

Unfortunately, the pedagogy of language is the larger half of all of man's intellectual enterprises and the thin filament of it to be followed through the maze must keep in view the landmarks pertinent to how that pedagogy has handled its basic purposes, including theft and deception. Language in its aural/oral aspects of detection, acquisition, replication must now shift to graphic forms. The signal/symbol powers of oral language must be mobilized to written forms. The pedagogy of reading requires acquisition of the graphic code and sequencing of its elements in symbolic patterns. The pedagogy will rest heavily on replicative powers such as echolalia and memorized recitation, with formulative powers such as original syntax long deferred sometimes indefinitely. The intense focus is replication, the distant hope and expectation, formulation.

The Graphic Revolution

The special application of signal detection that is reading, is based on matching an explicitly graphic pattern to stand for elements of the language as spoken. The heroic efforts to achieve acceptably accurate decoding and encoding of English is more easily understood when the complexities of the process are reviewed. The English alphabet is an old and odd conglomerate of forms with at best casual connections to language as spoken. Any one letter of the English alphabet may stand for several different sounds, two or more letters may share a single sound, some letters in some contexts are designated "silent" letters, all to the degree that if the sound system of English is to be studied, it is almost always done from a phonetic alphabet.

In addition, the signal to sound matching, already sufficiently irrational, evolved in the Western World arbitrary graphic forms such as printed letters, cursive, capitals, and lower case and systems of punctuation. Confronting the pedagogical realities, the academic mode most likely to win through the thickets of variables is heavy, even relentless, emphasis on detection, acquisition, and replication. The twenty-six-letter code must be instantly decodable in its non-phonetic multitude of orthographic variants. Otherwise word recognition would fail and there would be no forward motion toward decoding written syntax.

The verification of decoding was saying the word when seen, spelled orally, etc., then reading aloud on demand until each decoder could fuse pronunciation and syntax into exact lexical parallels to the printed page. Mercifully, most of us have long forgotten the anxieties the pedagogues induced and the pain of listening to peers struggle to read in the obvious absence of lexical fluency. Stories, poems, memory work, punctuation exercises, spelling bees (usually won as they still are by girls), altogether for most a charmless if necessary enterprise.

As the cognitive side of decoding gets underway, concurrent attention is given to graphic skills, the pedagogy of "penmanship." The penultimate step from oral/aural, ocular processing (reading) to wielding pen and pencil is ready to be taken. The fingers are now to learn arbitrary motions with surgical precision, fashioning arbitrary graphic shapes representing arbitrary speech elements in proper sequences. Several thousand words with infusions of new vocabulary. Names, places, numbers, all parts of speech, addressing syntax/grammar and idiom on the way. In retrospect, the "learning" that occurs is a near miracle. The passage from innate oral speech to the lexical skills was a quantum leap if there ever was one. It comes, however, at a cost.

The Literacy Spectrum

What does it mean to be able to read and write? The pedagogy is justified by the potential benefits the skills afford the individual and society. "Literacy: the state or quality of being literate." Literate: 1. able to read and write, 2. well-educated." Somewhere in the spectrum of literacy each new reader/writer falls. The evidence suggests that most fall exhausted. The pleasurable innate, oral language skills of speaking and listening had a rough passage through non-innate acquisition of competencies with the written word. Interminable copying, perpetual corrections, reading verification by paraphrase, and the tight focus on accuracy characterized the pedagogy to the almost total exclusion of communicative pleasures. The bright few went on ahead and became the well-educated. The preponderant majority learned to read and write. A hefty minority fails and continues to fail.

Even omitting immigrants from non-English speaking countries, the press assures us that our illiterates are counted in the tens of millions even though our educational efforts cost hundreds of billions. If millions are that badly off in workable reading and writing skills, many more millions must be in that twilight zone of the poorly educated despite acquisition of those same skills. Opinion testers frequently sample citizen responses to controversial issues. The testers know that responses are shaped by how the questions are phrased. Hence, "tested" public opinion must frequently be only the recycling of ignorance.

As history has succumbed to the trivia craze and theater to quiz shows, spin-offs and commercials, it was inevitable that Trivia II, or Whelp of Trivia would follow. The new short-cut to literacy is "Cultural Literacy": the 4500 words, phrases, names, dates and places "every American needs to know," by E.D. Hirsch, Jr. The complaint seems to be that students don't know anything and therefore reading about it is meaningless. As if the rich cognitions of our sundry realities can no longer enter the human central nervous system! Each normal child has a gigantic repository of data drawn from experience, as each has a linguistic system of fantastic inventive plasticity and creativity. Now we find there is nothing cohesive in the system. Imprecations!

It is too late for Hirsch's book. Television, rock, and our other directed educational system deserve the credit for this state of affairs. We continue to refer to grades 9-12 as "high." What, exactly, is the functional priority of these pedagogical settings? Training academy for college sports, training conservatory for some arts, driver training school, teen sex clinics, drug, alcohol, tobacco clinics, a context of social encounters, miscellaneous extracurricular activities, remedial classes, racial integrative busing, all inexorably migrating to the lower grades. The students know it's a fraud and rightly infer that education so conducted cannot be of any real importance. How can learning go on in such an uproar? It is not fair to expect students so busy in consuming what the schools offer to also acquire a veneer of culture. Hirsch and others will supply the veneer starting with words and phrases.

A fine education would entail modest costs although priceless in value. We have elected to spend very little on actual education. How often do we look closely and critically at how much is spent on litigation, administration, busing, and cabbing to integrate schools? And what is the grand total of costs of all school related activities not central to educational purposes? Deduct such costs and the remainder, if any, is the measure of our financial commitment to education. There is no mystery why the cost of "education" perpetually increases as the academic and intellectual competencies of students decline. It is not education that is expensive: its peripheral, parasitic enterprises are. The costs extend well beyond money. The losses must also be counted in the misdirected energies and efforts of the staff and the prostrate morale of faculty and students. The vested interests arrayed in favor of this status quo are many and powerful and include the very agencies that ought to be in opposition to it. Ditto for higher education.

Every eight to ten years the USA rediscovers "adult illiteracy." In 1979 the New York Times, under a Fred M. Hechinger byline, asked whether "America had written off writing ability." And the mail this day announced by brochure a Summer Writing Camp "for youths aged eight to sixteen who wish to combine learning with recreation." It is dedicated to fun and basic writing skills. The evidence is clear. If both reading and writing are not instituted early and precisely, the belated process of retrieval is laborious and millions fail. Thousands of illiterate athletes are admitted every year to institutions of higher education. When interviewed on TV or radio their impoverished vocabularies and primitive syntax confirm their misplacement in higher education. Which very naturally raises the ethical aspects of language pedagogy.

In the great concern for literacy, neither students nor mature adults should be singled or pluraled out for literate inadequacies. In the process of administrative evaluations of a university president and vice president, this writer chaired the solicitation and review of faculty and staff responses to a semi-formal questionnaire that provided a half-page for respondents' comments. Among several hundred returns, spelling and grammatical errors were common in about ten percent of them. Syntax was somewhat better, as it should have been, but irrationality, incoherence, lack of evidence, and sound argument comprised an even larger percentage--almost a third. Local academic frustrations could account for the strident emotional content but not the gross examples of marginal literacy. The worst faculty segment was, if anything, less literate than the average staff response. No one has dared to suggest that the professoriate be tested for literacy, presumably on the a priori grounds that as a body it would be the absolute model of whatever is best in literateness. It is clearly time for a national literacy test for school teachers from Harvard on down.

In the academic intensity and rigor that reading and writing require, where were the ethical concerns that might and should have threaded through the development of the skills? They were absent.

They are dropped out of deference to the purposes of a demanding pedagogy. Plagiarism is a hybrid of deception and theft according to sundry definitions of the concept. In the general development of the child, theft and deception receive concurrent attention in most households. In reading and writing pedagogy, where is ethics in the two major teaching modes? They are reading aloud orally to check pronunciation and syntax scanning and paraphrasing to confirm whether the reader has extracted the proper meanings from the printed page. Both usually are completely indifferent as to source recognition and to the paraphrasing that is essentially ideational copywork. The pedagogy of reading and writing are inherently deeply involved in unconscious, "innocent" plagiarism. The pedagogy permits, demands, and encourages all forms of usage of written materials. The ethics of acknowledgement is to be a later add-on to the processes of written exposition.

Deferred Expectations

The purpose of literacy is to arm the intellect of the individual; to afford greater mastery of the universe by enhanced discrimination among the realities and appearances that surround us. But only a minuscule few actually apply the hard-won skills of reading and writing to extracting the universe's secrets. Literacy as a tool is mostly all potential. The unrealized power of innate language, sensed subjectively as forever ready for great things, founders on the shoals of writing's formalities: spelling, vocabulary, syntax/grammar, and the rigors that ought to shape thought processes.

Language pedagogy is supposed to direct the student by shaping intelligence and motivation, inculcating culture and values from which the civilized citizen emerges. However, no matter to which manifestation attention is directed, literacy and language pedagogy at their best are but tools that in the absence of thought and ethics merely lead us more easily into irrationality and brutality. It is necessary to remind ourselves that in the 1930s and 1940s two of the most literate nations on earth were Germany and Japan. If such a massive pedagogical failure can occur, all other failures are rendered insignificant by comparison. But aren't all failures composites of thought and ethics? Not to exclude scholarship?

Literacy is the precursor of scholarship. Not many frank illiterates embark on plagiaristic ventures. It is rather a disorder of the quite well-informed and well-educated. Literacy can be thought of as the maturation of thought processes launched by inner speech transactions. We modify ourselves and the local universe by the models lexical skills provide. Although it is useful and instructive to resort to myths, oral history, song and story, graphic pedagogy supplies irresistible reference points for concepts and ideas. Not immutable points, but focal points for pragmatic/semantic analysis. Something strange is going on in this part of the galaxy. The universe has found a way to model itself by lexical skills, as the innate supersystem speeds the graphic/symbolic revolution.

Print lingers. It even comes back to haunt as will and do computers' symbolic memories. Durability and replication of graphic, electronic codes invite both reflection and revision. The transient context of the spoken word is easily mitigated. The printed word or its equivalent tends to assume the nature of a permanent contract. Ideas, words, sentences, phrases become the objectives of scholarship and symbolic processes in operation create commodities out of meanings.

IV

LANGUAGE AND SCHOLARSHIP

In the humanities and liberal arts language is the primary and, in some instances, the exclusive tool of scholarship. The extraction of laws, formulae, and equations of the hard sciences should not be considered "mere" extensions of the common linguistic code. Some realities are perhaps forever reserved for mathematic conceptualization alone. But the significance of such "realities," condensed, diluted, extrapolated, requires resort to academic rhetoric, polemics, and seemingly endless exposition. What is scholarship aside from whatever scholars are doing?

Implicit in the concept of scholarship and the behaviors of scholarly practitioners is the idea that research, analysis, and synthesis can validate the laws, principles, and processes underlying anything and everything. Also implicitly are the notions that formal disciplines are required to advance knowledge and understanding such as logic, experimentation, hypothesis testing, statistical inference, test re-test confirmation, and accumulation of new data and new facts on which the cycle continues moving into the yet unknown or imperfectly understood. In effect, scholarly research consists of ideas about the generation of ideas. But naturally, scholars, even though sharing core consensus, eventually part company on the best or better modes for advancing knowledge. It is, for example, not clear whether knowledge is won more expeditiously by channeling efforts in canonical scholarly pursuits, or whether non-canonical inductive leaps bring investigators to more prompt and fruitful destinations.

It is treacherous, even arrogant, to attempt to characterize the entire scholarly enterprise. Such research extends from the largely polemical to the strictly quantitative. That to be determined by the researcher extends from hypothesis hunting to data sifting and testing. No one could with confidence pass judgment on the merit of content unless one has been working at the research borders of the subject matter involved. Further, there are many disciplines and most are compelled to reach into other disciplines to better understand their own as particle physics and astrophysics have revolutionized each other by mutual enrichment. The critic must be able to reach across disciplines.

Exposition derived from rigorous quantification is often extracted reluctantly. Its validity of content usually exists almost exclusively in its mathematical form. Great care is exercised in avoiding unwarranted extrapolations. In most forms of polemical research, quantified data are used in supporting hypotheses. The ideas are all derivative. The cumulative effect must be original to a limited degree. The limit is set by the derivative nature of practically all of the major ideas. Many minds have been over the same thoughts before, but the distribution of those thoughts and the verbal forms of them must constitute some measure of originality. Some, but probably not much. So even if all of the sentences are original and all of the paragraphs, the claims of originality are greatly attenuated by the common core of ideas on which all of us are obliged to draw. Yet if this monograph is published and copyrighted, it is a candidate for plagiarism, and if proved, the miscreant plagiarist or infringer can be punished.

Practically all original scientific theories have been proved false. What we remember are the valid few that have survived. Not even the magnificent synthesis of Newton remained untouched. Scientific theories are born to die the deaths of invalidity. Who remembers Ptolemy's Theory? The theorist is lucky to be remembered for the useful dismemberment of his theory. In the most rigorous of the sciences, the odds against the original theory being valid are prohibitive and intimidating. Wild theories such as plate tectonics, black holes, neutron stars, quasars, quarks, and Big Bang come to mind as original hypotheses enroute to conclusive verification explaining and destroying earlier constructs in the process. Part of the problem of originality appears to be excessive conservatism.

The truth about the pursuit of truth is that most of the original, when it is indeed original, is probably false, and much of it certainly false. That some of it is true may be only contingently so. That appears to be the way it is in the hard sciences. Is there a reason to believe that truth is more easily achieved in the "behavioral sciences?" Practically everything published in the behavioral sciences is considered to be "original" work. There is no evidence that the index of validity is higher in the behavioral sciences than the physical sciences. The "experts" in psychology, history, economics, are the "authorities" who certify the "originality" of scholarship in their respective disciplines. Those experts cannot always be certifying the validity of the original materials. Usually they certify only that the work is original not that the content is a definitive truth. How else are their ubiquitous contradictory findings to be explained or their chronic inability to confirm the findings of others?

Originality develops its own orthodoxy. A new truth can never be orthodox. The arbiters of research consist of peers whose task is to review new research. The averaged judgment of peers becomes the monitor of--of what? Originality or truth? It is far easier to find the quantum of originality than the quantum of truth. The quantum of truth is a leap. The quantum of originality is a featureless continuum. There isn't much evidence that small originalities glide imperceptibly into truths, small or large.

The issue of validity and truth, central to the issue of plagiarism, is rarely raised. The value of scholarship must exist in its validity as a scholarly contribution or in its convertibility into some kind of asset. Expropriating the words and ideas of another cannot be much of an offense if those words and ideas are inconsequential. Is the assumption true that simply because some words and ideas are original they are therefore of equivalent value to words and ideas that constitute new truths?

The Scholarly Context

Not all scholarship and research transpires on college campuses. It would seem plausible that the sheer mass of what purports to be scholarship in action is campus generated. There are obviously many powerful and productive research centers associated with colleges. But few are exempt from the balancing acts of serving broad institutional objectives, usually defined as <u>teaching</u>, <u>service</u>, and <u>research</u> with emphasis usually in that order for primarily political reasons and because the reward system is tied to the triad.

The paragon who can excel in teaching brilliantly, publishing profusely, and servicing important constituencies does not have to worry about the vagaries of the reward system. The broad professoriate does worry and does not consist of many paragons. The preponderant majority must fashion a workable parlay from the three expectations, sometimes concentrating on two out of the three, or doing such exemplary work that only one of the three is sufficient for higher level rewards, that is, salary, tenure, and promotion recognition. On the scholarly side, the "publish or perish" cliche has lost much of its force in most college settings as renewed emphasis was placed on teaching, partly in response to student demands of the sixties and seventies.

Despite proliferation of journals, competition for limited publishing space borders on the ferocious. The peer refereed journal evolved to assure high standards of research and to avoid various species of bias. In theory, the peer editorial panels were to determine whether the submitted research documents were original, valid, and consequential. Research could be true, but of little consequence. Research could be original, even interesting, but invalid. Research ought to be both valid and consequential. Research should earn its originality by being both valid and consequential. In practice, peer panels themselves are subject to methodological and intellectual orthodoxies that result in the strange advice offered by the <u>Research Highlights</u> cited above. Not surprising when the nature of committee deliberations is understood. The committee was contrived to find the least common denominator of mental operations. The result is a composite of current research ideologies.

Because the scholarly accomplishments will be marginal and short of "the grand synthesis," the products are known to be transient. Polemical scholarship then becomes an exercise in <u>fastness</u> and <u>firstness</u>. Publishing urgency pushes scholarship toward the <u>original</u>. There are hundreds of journals with publishing deadlines to meet and thousands of scholars contesting for places in them. If members of the professoriate do not appear with some regularity in the journals of established academic quality, nothing much persuasive appears on the resumes and vitae. The "publish or perish" cliche not only acknowledges the climate in which scholarship proceeds but suggests as well that it is not the producer alone that is perishable but the product as well.

Scholarship as Elitism

Scholarship is inherently an intellectual enterprise perpetually at war with those in the anti-intellectual camp. There is no doubt that foolish things are done in the name of scholarship and that it has had its share of palpable frauds. More than other enterprises, the discipline of scholarship is to a high degree self-correctable. Recent anti-intellectual forces moved under the banner of anti-elitism. The idea of an intellectual elite was repugnant. In the totally egalitarian universe there was to be no claim to superiority in curriculum, academic performance, or research values. Students were peers of the professors. Curriculum was judged on relevance, academic performance on improvement, admissions open to all, and as some were inclined to say, "irregardless."

The inclination to bend every enterprise to political/ideological ends results in strange distortions, even contortions, of scholarship. Each contending faction wants its own scholarship and its own curriculum. Parochial interests have created pedagogies for racism, sexism, ageism, etc., as if the entire scholarly enterprise and all of its ways were a gigantic conspiracy against the group concerned. Black studies, Hispanic studies, women's studies, curricula detached from the intellectual main stream may be good political strategy and ego gratifying, but the potential trap is that all will find exactly what they want to see and soon each will be paraphrasing within their own orthodoxy and will drift, as has so much of scholarship, away from validity and significance. After the close paraphrase looms the temptation to plagiarize. What is as anti-intellectual as plagiarism? The ideological chants of "educated" constituencies.

Scholarship Goes Worldly

Higher education has now so many gods before it that its prime purpose has become to perpetuate itself and prosper under the academic banners of teaching, service, and research (largely in that order). The intense search for the original has supplanted the rigorous pursuit of validity and the relentless pursuit of truth. The road to truth is through validity: the strength, cohesiveness of evidence, and the insight that discerns the laws presumed to be shaping the data. Unfortunately, truth has no natural constituency. It is indifferent to the political and social consequences that it might have. Truth is almost always socially unacceptable until it is grudgingly canonized by the culture that has exhausted its resistance to it. Finally, even Galileo gets a pontifical embrace. All new truths must slice their way into a resistant body of interlocked, convoluted beliefs. We would rather believe than prove. Paradoxically, only pure idealists are intellectually committed to the reality and realism of tested truths.

The scholarly ideal tends to be singular while our pragmatic non-scholarly values are many and seductive. Any value external to the scholarly ideal is capable of subverting it. The irresistible human tendency to drift to ideology, the push/pull of publishing needs, author and publisher, peer review circularity, the short half-life of polemical research, and the bend and tilt of commercial exploitation.

It is quite reasonable to raise the issue whether research motivated by fastness and firstness is consistent with the objectives of determining truth and significance. Given the state of the behavioral sciences much of the effort must be polemical; research ideas cast in rhetorical forms that set up concepts to be explored and tested. A premium is placed on current understandings that become a kind of current axiology. Polemical research therefore requires paraphrasic skills of a high order, first to represent the known and canonical with fidelity, secondly, to differentiate source materials from "original" matter.

As scholarship became institutionalized and bureaucratized, the formal reward system was erected: salary, promotion, tenure, upward professional mobility, administration, prestige, perks, fringe benefits, copyrights, royalties, consultancies, and even local or national fame. In short, the academy followed the corporate model. The profession's reward system was uncoupled from "scholarship for its own sake" and slipped into bed with commercial aspirations. It was no longer money *or*, but money *and*, fame, immortality. The heavily subsidized intellectual life finally arrived. The work of the mind could compete to a degree with the performances of muscles, the impulses of glands, and the primitive cunning of politics. What was once the satisfaction of beneficially influencing another mind or sensitizing another mind to new ideas and aspects of the world of intellect has been other directed by more worldly concerns.

"Virtue is its own reward" we are told. Which we must admit never was much of an inducement for us. But it is a good place to start. The reward for meritorious scholarship must start with the intellectual gratification of the accomplishment. There is scholarship for its own sake that intellects do for the same reason that some people climb mountains. The challenge is to extend matters to new extremities. But only a few strange idealists labor in the academic vineyards indifferent to public acclaim. Even in the academy the labors are rarely those of metaphoric love. There are many laboring in the academic vineyards but only the vintners have the alchemy necessary to sanctify the academic wines.

V

ACADEMIC ETHICS

There are many ways to approach the question of academic ethics. One obvious way is to review behaviors of scholars, the professoriate, and academic administrators--a kind of ethics at the source, and then review the larger arena of the behaviors of the well educated, ethics in the fields of non-academic endeavors. <u>Time</u> magazine's May 25, 1987 cover story, "Whatever Happened to Ethics?" starts with a Walter Shapiro byline, a highly alliterative, cliche-ridden, sanctimonious romp through the failings of others leading to the strong suggestion that the fault is that of Ronald Reagan for not setting better examples of probity in office. The second paragraph ends with the useless rhetorical question, "Put bluntly, has the mindless materialism of the '80s left in its wake a values vacuum?" The vacuity is in not asking the right questions and in hustling a scape-goat, RWR, for the individual failings of the highly educated upper echelons of our society. There is really only one game in town, power and money, and it is played without any moral or ethical encumbrances. As the "wheelers and dealers" so honestly expressed it, power is the game and money is how the score is kept. Is there much difference as our ethical inquiry shifts to the colleges and universities?

By considerable contrast there is Allan Bloom's <u>Closing of the American Mind</u>, an extended, descriptive indictment of the products of higher education, extrapolating its failures by assessment of student values. This is a little closer to actual matters than <u>Time</u> magazine's salivating, almost joyous revelations of our unethical selves. What has happened that we are now both amoral and mentally shackled? The colleges and universities, the scholars and professoriate have abandoned truth, discipline, prudence, merit, the old ideals and virtues as basically fraudulent in favor of "constituent" ideologies.

The Core Truth

They have forgotten that the core of all principle must be truth. Even the core of ethics starts with truth. The object of all education is the pursuit of truth. The Great Assumption is that the human mind is capable of validating truth and, if necessary, enduring it. Courage, discipline, and resolution determine truth; courage, discipline, and resolution sustain it. As an abstract matter, the human species simply does not have much commitment to truth. We prefer to be governed by polite and convenient self-serving fictions, rationalizations, and disinformation. Our culture has lost the passion for truth and the conviction that it exists, that it has some kind of demonstrable reality. Yet if we do not press on to new truths, we risk the danger of becoming intellectual caricatures of ourselves. The academy, like the world at large, is now inhabited by true believers not truth pursuers.

Comparative Ethics

In the absence of categorical evidence, there is no reason to assume academic ethics is better than business ethics, political ethics, religious ethics, or any other arena claiming to observe ethical considerations. There is some reason to expect academic ethics to be better because of the academy's presumed dedication to pursuing truth wherever the evidence leads, and to do it by formal, open, verifiable procedures.

The notion of ethics had a twin source in philosophy and religion and reconciling ethics to individual and group behaviors best demonstrates the ambivalence that has persisted since the invention of sin. All groups persist in thinking of themselves in morally acceptable terms but are reluctant or even adamant in granting equal ethics to other groups. Deep within the notion of ethics is the model of the individual or group completely and totally ethical in all matters great and small, the individual that you can trust with your pocketbook, your wife, your children, your home, your honor. Our national model, Abe Lincoln, was not famous for being selectively honest, worrying about his "image" or concerned about his "credibility." The only real issue is how far we have slipped from the model and why.

A number of converging influences have been at work: the relativity of situational ethics, the democratizating of education, and intrusion of ideology into scholarship. The course from truth and axiom to dogma and dogmatism has been greased by self-interest. Those individuals and groups committed to the money/power game are supposed to be especially vulnerable to temptation. Yet stock brokers, clergymen, corporate executives, and labor leaders probably all have the same basic incidence of "falling from grace." The fall out of ethics is, however, dramatized by the heights from which the fall is precipitated. Which confirms the disadvantaged and underprivileged in their less spectacular failings.

Ethics in government and politics, as with all other areas, requires the revival of the classic rhetorical term <u>oxymoron</u> that can be defined by familiar examples--athletic scholarship, military intelligence, honest politician, disarmament conference, the United Nations, etc. Should academic ethics join that group of compounds comprised of internal contradictions?

A very good case can be made that it should. The press, the scholars, the college "educated" now fully appreciate that the world is composed of "constituencies," that is, subgroups with extremely parochial interests. There is no majority. There are only minorities with deliverable majorities. Each minority is the custodian of its own truths, i.e., dogmas. No minority dogmas can be questioned. To question a minority dogma is to be "insensitive." To provide evidence counter to the dogma will provoke the appropriate label--racist, sexist, elitist, leftist, rightist, pacifist, militarist, and there is an "ist" to fit all contingencies.

Scholars know that the function of the human nervous system is to discriminate for which certain kinds of sensitivities are required. Both functions are essential in the intellectual process. Both terms have been mobilized as shibboleths in the political process. For some years now, the college educated community has expressed grave concern about the "images" of things, the campus, the city, the school, their officers, the "image" of the professoriate. Likewise, their credibility. Does no one care that "image" has substituted for such values as maturity, judgment, honor? That "credibility" has substituted for honesty, integrity, wholeness? Why worry about whether a politician or a professor is "believable" and whether other people will perceive them as believable? Is this not a blatant admission that we do not know and do not expect that either, as a practical matter, will be honest? Therefore, it is best to worry whether the credulous will be satisfied. It is only necessary to preserve the appearances of honesty. Is he/she a "credible" candidate? One can strive in vain to find a happy explanation for these compulsive, meaningless rituals. Bloom is right. The mind is closed.

The scholars flock to the political ideologies and ideational niches of the intellectual ecologies. Political, economic, cultural, social, psychological pundits crowd the marketplace of "opinion." Practically never does the opinion purveyor caution the consumer that the writer or speaker has a constituency in mind, is paid well to address that constituency, and has strong vested interests in the form of unacknowledged biases. No claim is made of objectivity or to commitment to truth. In truth, the "opinion" pages are intrinsically "opinionated." All editorial pages should have a headed disclaimer, "You will find very little truth herein."

Should the scholarly have better ethics than other agencies? A good argument can be made that they should. Scholars still justify and demand the shield of tenure. The purpose of tenure was to afford scholars the right to determine and disseminate truth as conscientious research and study revealed it, and to protect them in that search from disapproving and possibly vengeful ideologies.

In a new publication, Academic Computing, Spring 1987, Vol. 1, No. 1, there is an article by Phillip and Carol Cartwright, Pennsylvania State University, titled, "Software Development: Considerations for Promotion and Tenure." The thesis is that "software development" ought to have its proper place and weighting in tenure consideration. It is the concept of tenure that is arresting. "Tenure is job security only in the sense that it provides the foundation for intellectual risk-taking and free inquiry and, in that way, facilitates the creation and transmission of knowledge. Thus, the major utility of the tenure system, both for the individual and the institution, is safeguarding academic freedom." "Free inquiry," "academic freedom," nothing of the responsibility to tell the truth and the hazards thereof. The "risk-taking" is all intellectual, not moral. Nothing on the moral obligations of tenure. The protection of tenure, it is contended, should be extended to information processors, not confined to the truth seekers.

The nation and the educated have been obsessed with rights for about two decades to the almost total exclusion of responsibilities, values, and truth. The rights of labor, farmers, minorities, felons, the incarcerated, the indigent, fetuses, animals, stockholders, children, the handicapped, the addicted, homosexuals, the diseased, the mentally incompetent, the illegal alien, refugees, etc. If it was Henry Ford who said the business of America was business, now the business of the United States is the merchandising of universal rights, with the inevitable consequences of making the country one vast refugee camp of minority natives and foreigners. Unfortunately, those few who remain "minding the store," those responsible for producing goods and rendering essential services, the productive, useful minority diminishes, and the per capita wealth of the nation decreases. The decline of the United States does coincide with the internal political "movements," turmoil of contending ideologies, and the largely tacit agreement among constituencies not to call attention to any inconvenient truths about each other. A rights gridlock is coming fast.

Truth and Tenure

For a while in the sixties and seventies a small minority of rather emphatic academic voices were objuring the rights of tenure on principle. The majority voice continued to prevail with the traditional defenses of the otherwise quite extraordinary right of tenure. If there is no longer a conviction that scholars could delineate unpleasant truths, there is no discernible justification for the career-long security that tenure provides. To demand the right of tenure with no commitment to truth is blatantly intellectually dishonest. The chain of logic, given the primary assumption, takes this kind of shape:

If you believe in tenure, you believe in truth. If you believe that knowledge carefully derived is valid, you believe in truth. If you claim to be a teacher or accept the title of professor, you believe in truth. If nothing is true, we don't need teachers, professors, or schools. If there is no truth, then there is no knowledge. The science of epistemology has failed. If there is no knowledge, all of education is a delusion. Then traditional tests of knowledge, evidence, logic, observation, critical analysis, hypothesis testing are all fraudulent and useless. If this is the state that we have reached, then all of education is a total waste of time, effort, and money.

There is no purpose in training intellects to spread nonexistent knowledge. We must therefore conclude as axiomatic that the function of higher education is to determine the truth and share it. My ultimate objection to university aims and objectives statements is that they do not believe in truth, merit, values, or ethics. The new academic religion of relevance, productivity, and relativity writes our aims and objectives for us.

What has become of truth? We are learning new truths about truth. It is too valuable to be wasted by telling it. Truth is a devastating weapon, especially if it never needs using. Truth is frequently too dangerous to vested interests to be safely revealed. Another good reason for suppressing it. Truth is always dangerous to someone's interests. The truth is, we now know, there is no compelling need to tell it just because someone knows it. Gratuitous truth telling is completely out of fashion. It must be carefully shaped to parochial interests. No one, it appears, has a vested interest in the truth just because it is true. Truth no longer has a natural constituency. Scholarship used to be its primary constituency. A corollary truth is that the academy doesn't want the truth about it known, especially its lost interest in truth. It is here that the diagnostic therapeutics of Doctors Bennett, Boyer and Bloom and many others neglect to address the spectacular failures of education in the United States.

Sins of the Academy

Sloth, incompetence, and fraud account for practically all of the academic sins. Cheating on examinations. Buying term papers. Faking data. Padding vitae. Copying. A basic discovery of humankind was that work was laborious and merit painfully slow to accumulate. As one wag observed, "If work is all that good, why do people have to be paid to do it?" The problem is to make it appear that the academic work has been properly accomplished. The whole world might play this fraudulent game, but when it is played in the academy dedicated to truth, knowledge and principles, the offense is a mortal wound to the intellectual enterprise.

Unfortunately, the academy itself is responsible for most of its own sins. There is a morbid, egocentric side of all intellectualisms that has led to a movement best described as anti-elitism. All other enterprises are permitted their elite. In higher education it is suspect. On the record, the claims of higher education clearly suggest a gross inclination to over-value itself. Higher education as a way of life. Publish or perish! Pass or fail! Credential or languish! Higher education improves the quality of life! Higher education makes the individual an important person. Academic attainment becomes, in some instances, a life or death matter. In the Big Ten, suicides clustered around mid-semester and final examination time. Japanese students who dishonored family and ancestors by academic failures would often choose self-extinction. Grade inflation has probably saved more lives than academic rigor has ever cost.

Not all sinning in the academy is academic. Envy, greed, character assassination, gossip, lying, conniving, etc., made uglier by being the product of brighter minds, presumably more mature. No one quantifies these offenses. Verbal and sexual harassment are not new offenses, just offenses that the civil rights movement has recently dramatized. What did the cynical world expect would happen when lascivious, old men called professors were placed in academic power over nubile, lovely maidens called coeds? Or now, lascivious older women in academic power over handsome young studs? And it is typical now to treat each newly discovered old social pathology as "just the tip of the iceberg."

Brutal, nasty things go on in the academy all the time. One is constantly surprised that there is so much of it and so much of it is so bad. It is not entirely a myth that eighty percent of the gossip on the grapevine is true . . . and one can be sure that much of the venality is never ventilated at all. Well known campus characters function as focal points of gossip transmission and they probably serve some social cathartic purpose on the internal side.

What the external world sees are the efforts of campus public relations officers assigned to "image building." Schools worry far more about their image and credibility than they do about morale, morals, and integrity. That an institution of higher education would condescend to address seriously anything as superficial as image is a depressing index to how far the academy has allowed the world to dictate its standards and objectives.

The Chronicle of Higher Education quantifies and charts multiple indices to the state of higher education, mostly budgets and finance, followed by administrative problems, followed by curriculum, and lesser matters such as teaching, academic governance, collective bargaining, with most pages allocated to administrative job placement. Somewhere, some higher educational publication should become a clearing house for recording and reporting all academic crimes and misdemeanors committed by academics great and small, students and staff, and, especially, faculty and administration. The inquiry should start at the top and work its way down to college athletics.

If expressed concern means anything, faculty morale, nationwide, has yet to find its absolute bottom. Attributions of blame spread in all directions. Remedies spew forth from as many directions. Politicians and fiscal conservatives smugly remind the academy that as the educational expenditures go up, student competencies go down. Everyone knows something is gravely wrong but no one is sure exactly what. Suspicion builds that higher education has become a vast, expensive charade in which image is the stimulus and posturing is the response. The academy still purports to believe in academic crime and punishment and it will still go through the motions even though its claim to moral superiority has been tarnished by its own ethical and intellectual failings. Will academic ethics ever revive? Not until the professoriate is adamantly recommitted to truth, principle, discipline, equity and responsibility, and so demonstrates in technical, professional, political, and personal matters.

Academic Crime and Punishment

For general offenses, disgrace and/or dismissal. For academic high crimes and misdemeanors, banishment. For lesser offenses, lesser punishments--suspension or reprimands. Plagiarism is an academic capital offense, punishable by academic death for student or faculty. With or without warnings. Faculty are supposed to know better having acquired through training, a lucid, explicit notion of what constitutes plagiarism. The well known penalties to function as stiff inhibitors that would keep all academics about their honest labors. Not likely. The temptation to use short cuts is strong. An academic tenured appointment is a clean, safe, honorific, relatively unstressful, well paying job when all perks and collaterals are figured in, i.e., sabbaticals, summer pay, frequent holidays, consultancy fees, royalties, and employment for life. Those who moan about low salaries in higher education rarely pass around certified copies of their latest IRS filing to prove relative poverty.

Students are dismissible for any form of demonstrable cheating. Much talent and genius are expended on modes of successful cheating and on modes to frustrate successful cheating. The net result, we may safely assume, is a stand-off with probably somewhat more cheating undetected than apprehended. Examinations provide acute crises driving students to desperate extremities. Term paper deadlines provoke panic in the academic groves. An authoritative book on cheating in higher education would be a monument to creatively avoiding known scholarly obligations and discovering original forms of undetectable deceptions. The student who cheats is supposed to understand that he/she is cheating oneself. In this view, if virtue is its own reward, sloth and cheating are their own punishments.

As a greater percentage of the population presents itself for higher education, the average level of intellectual potential must drop assuming that intelligence potential is not advancing biologically. If it is advancing, it is hard to explain the decline in academic skills and the dramatic advance in athletic performance in recent decades. Some sort of inverse, or even perverse, relationship possibly? It was not an accident that Southern California's football program was "disciplined" by the NCAA. Was the program banished from the campus? In the modern era, football programs are never banished from the campus. A higher premium is placed on football than academic ethics and integrity. It could and has been observed that football has absolutely nothing to do with higher education except that it happens on college campuses. It therefore is held to its own ethics, which is to say, no ethics. But is the academic side any better?

Individual students are sporadically dismissed for cheating on exams or plagiarizing term papers. Yet an academic spin-off enterprise has developed that offers ghost written term papers on any major subject, prices quoted per page, references, and a bibliographic addenda. Posted in conspicuous places on lecture hall bulletin boards. But statistics of offenses are not kept. Today, if a student cheats, it is much more likely that the student will hire a lawyer who will demonstrate that if his client had been properly taught to read and write his client would not have been obliged to cheat or plagiarize. Besides:

> It is the school's fault for placing my client on the football team without those skills. Nowhere in the school catalogue or bulletin does it stipulate that the student must be able to read and write to matriculate or play on the football team. The terms <u>reading</u> and <u>writing</u> do not even appear in the bulletin's index as a requirement for admission. I rest my case.

You don't have to be able to read and write in most colleges but you can be nicked for plagiarism. Sounds a little like entrapment, doesn't it?

The insert below is largely self-explanatory. For every Jeff Burger exposed how many might we estimate remain unexposed? A flyer from a new publication is directed to and titled <u>The Teaching Professor</u>. It promises to assist the professor's art of pedagogy in a variety of ways to achieve the ever elusive "teaching excellence" increasingly stipulated as a tenure criterion. One of the areas of assistance offered is a slice of ethics. "Encourage academic integrity among the 56 percent of college students who plan to cheat on at least one major test or assignment in college." Certainly a fascinating statistic that might lead the morbidly curious to ask what the percentage was that planned to cheat all of the time or most of the time. What was the average expected incidence of planned cheating? It appears that more than half planned on cheating based on need and/or opportunity.

> [Compiled by Mike Smith, St. Louis Post-Dispatch Deputy Sports Editor, August 21, 1987] Brouhaha at Bo Jackson U.: An "academic honesty" committee at Auburn recently voted to suspend quarterback Jeff Burger for plagiarizing a class report. But Burger found a sympathetic ear in a school vice president, who lifted the suspension on the ground that Burger already had suffered enough through all the newspaper publicity over the plagiarism and over an arrest for public intoxication and carrying a concealed weapon.
>
> A reader brought all this up to Los Angeles Times columnist Scott Ostler and asked him if he thought justice had been served. Ostler wrote:
>
> "I think justice has been tweaked in the fanny. But before I evaluate how much Burger has suffered from reading about himself in the newspapers, I have to know more facts--such as whether or not he can read. This is Auburn, remember.
>
> "As for the vice president, this guy should have been Jack the Ripper's attorney. Jack would have got off with 100 hours of community service."

Is this not a curious situation? The marginally literate are invited into higher education with, at best, limited skills in paraphrasing and are expected to do original work, the very work that almost half of the faculty eschews. The expectations are unrealistic. The orthodox notion of plagiarism is an invitation to the entrapment of the student. At a time when student "rights" have vastly outrun student responsibilities, it is not likely that there will be an orgy of complaints of student plagiarism. Perhaps it is just as well. It is at least an area ripe with potential for confusion, abuse, and capriciousness. Nor does the threat of punishment, rarely applied, add one whit to the student's competencies in exposition, original or otherwise.

The punishment is stern, the rationale confused, and the equity questionable. It is the rare college president who doesn't use a ghost writer. On most campuses if you use "the written or oral work of another without acknowledging the source," you have plagiarized. Presumably, the college president doesn't need the practice of writing any longer. Or for that matter, the thinking that goes into writing. The students, poor dears, wouldn't dare raise this objection. But their lawyers wouldn't hesitate. One object of college is to encourage students to read extensively, recall efficiently, and write coherently on potentially quite difficult matters. The plagiarism warning looks good in the catalogue, if indeed it appears in the catalogue, but it accomplishes nothing.

Let us turn now to the faculty handbook, if there is one. It may caution scholars about plagiarism but frequently does not because scholars are supposed to know how repugnant the academic community regards the act of plagiarism. Moreover, the ethics of scholars are assumed to be so much better than the non-academic laity that such offenses would be improbable on the face of it. The temptations must therefore be largely reserved for students and creative writers. Yet, every few weeks or months a new plagiarism case breaks into the news.

We academics are forever carving up the expositions of others, paraphrasing here, copying there, and printing, publishing, and distributing words, phrases, ideas, sentences, paragraphs "not our own." We explain that much of the exposition that we process or re-process is in the academic public domain. I once wrote the articles and by-laws that became a formally accepted governance charter. After some minor revisions, it was reported out to the faculty as a committee document. It served for ten years, undergoing almost annual revision. So far as I know, no one ever acknowledged the source. Nor did I ever expect the original source to be acknowledged. Nor the appearance in administrative memos of portions of my more casual bouts of exposition. Plagiarism is a highly situational offense. We have all profited by copying and paraphrasing, some more than others. Claiming credit for authoring a common enough governance charter doesn't do much for a professor's vita. Even if the document is original, significant, and valid.

The notion that punishment is a cure for plagiarism is about as sound as the notion that punishment cures anything. Punishment certainly inhibits some but leaves others completely undeterred. Since we find in punishment a most inexact behavioral science, the severity of the punishment for plagiarism is difficult to justify, especially with students. Nor should punishment of faculty for plagiarism go its largely unexamined way.

The young, bright and sensitive, especially, show signs of becoming cynical about both ethics and punishment. Thousands of college students borrow millions of federal dollars for tuition and other college costs with no intention whatever of repaying the loans. Presumably, if plagiarism is punishable, there are ethical reasons, sound ethical reasons, that support it. When we look to the punishments for far more drastic forms of unethical behavior, we have reasons for cynicism.

An Academic Capital Crime

If asked whether plagiarism represents an example of unethical behavior, practically all scholars would promptly and fervently offer assent, whether the offense occurred in academic matter or any other form of written exposition. Such response would be taken as evidence of academic ethics.

If plagiarism is considered an academic offense against intellectual ethics, it is only fair to examine the moral fabric of higher education as it is and as it purports to be. It borders on the quaint to employ such a term as <u>sin</u>. Our society doesn't much believe in sin any more and if there is anything left of it, the mores of plagiarism is a good place to look. Sins, wrongs, offenses, torts, whatever the terminology we continue to act and function as if we believed in sin as rooted in the human condition. We also are supposed to believe in humane treatment of offenders.

We would destroy the academic careers of students and faculty for plagiarism, real or alleged, however it is defined, but all around us, on campus and off, flagrant unethical behaviors receive bemused tolerance. Extenuating factors are used as rationalizations. The fault lies in society and the system. All sins are relative. Not so with plagiarism.

Plagiarism requires proper placing in the realm of academic crimes and punishments and in the context of the special niche written exposition and originality occupy in the processes of higher education. In Lindey's book on plagiarism, reviewed earlier, it was from law that his investigations provided understandings of plagiarism in literature, art and music. The law illuminated plagiarism as a legal offense in only the most general way. The law did not turn inward to press the issues raised by the legal definitions of plagiarism. The several legal definitions, almost paraphrases of each other, remained untouched and were treated as sufficiently explicit for purposes of making legal representations of wrongs and for formal adjudication of those wrongs. The critical analysis of Lindey was essentially deductive. Plagiarism was what the courts said it was, as one might assume. But plagiarism per the courts was not what the legal definitions said it was. Lindey never suggested that the legal definitions might well profit by revision in the light of the many court decisions that he reviewed.

Lindey is an excellent source for avoiding plagiarism in music and literature. Alex Haley, charged with plagiarism, and who settled out of court, might have profited by reading it. But the scholar would misplace his trust if his understanding embraced only the legal model.

VI

ACADEMIC EQUITY AND DEBT

The crux of plagiarism is who owes what to whom and why. Moral and intellectual debts accumulate quickly while paying them off can become laborious or even hazardous. It is assumed that scholars to be scholars must not only engage in persistent study but must also share their intellectual achievements by offering them to the broadest academic community through publication. It is the first and primary obligation, or debt of the scholar. The scholar has other obligations. In addition to what they are supposed to do, scholars receive a substantial subsidy through state or private agencies to practice their elected profession. They are, in effect, paid well, on the whole, for spending their lives in the most agreeable way: intellectual pursuits.

Scholars have a further indebtedness in the trust society places in them to teach and guide younger minds in the educational process. The largest obligation is imposed by the granting of tenure for scholarly achievement. Not only does the scholar enjoy the intellectual good life but is given a sinecure in the academic vineyard. How jealously protective can the scholars justifiably be of their published achievements?

In practice, quite protective, as it turns out. Proper acknowledgements may heighten a scholar's feelings of self-worth. It is gratifying to note that another scholar appreciates your work. Nor are scholars any more free of insecurities than any other professional. There is a touch of bravado in calling yourself a professor. Some of that insecurity is justified by the reality that most scholarly achievements must, by their nature, be modest not electrifying.

The Public's Goods?

But whose works are those? We must ask again what is the purpose of scholarship if it is not to have new knowledge enter the public domain. Creative writing, invention, artistry are not at issue, except as those efforts may occasionally overlap scholarship. It could be argued that inasmuch as society subsidizes scholars in the pursuits that they have elected, their products and achievements, one and all, belong to the society that subsidizes them and belong especially to their peers working the same intellectual stratum.

Aside from the conventionalized notions that there is such an act as plagiarism and that the act is one of the dimensions of intellectual dishonesty, how fundamental is the debt of current scholarship to prior scholarly achievements? Most would say profound inasmuch as one "flows" from the other. It is, indeed, one grand stream.

The pursuit of intellectual indebtedness is actually the study of the accretion of intellect, knowledge and understanding in the individual's development. Deep are the roots and endless the indebtedness. Scholarly attainments are in part a product of sophisticated use of the language itself. Parents, schools, and teachers in their sundry efforts--superb, indifferent or inept--shape the usually tortuous course to magazines, books, journals, libraries, wherever we paused to read, browse, and think. What determined what adhered to long term memory and what short term memory filtered out? We must also include laic discourses, trite, wise, perceptive, dogmatic, of relatives, friends, peers, and strangers.

The informal indebtedness appears absolute until we remind ourselves that incipient scholars are also self-made by predilections induced by both intelligence and background. To some, it comes as a surprise or even shock to discover that one is an autonomous thinker and that thinking and learning are instruments of revelation and that out there are accumulations to be made at only the cost of effort. The intellectual universe is mine, however mean my material one. Later we work our way by imperceptible gradations to the archaic formal rules of crediting sources. Our informal indebtedness that is part of the intellectual awakening later becomes a semi-formal and then formal ethical obligation.

To what are scholars really entitled? Most would answer recognition for strong, solid, creative work, namely scholarship that is both valid in content and of intellectual import, and the kind of recognition that would offset the several forms of obligations on the other side of scholarship, the users. While the public has a clear and broad claim to the products of scholarship, the active scholars have obligations to themselves that are moral, intellectual, even sentimental, when prior sources are drawn upon. Nor should the obligation of common or uncommon courtesy be neglected.

What can we use? What do we use? Where and when does abuse start? In equity and ethics, scholars are entitled to recognition for their research accomplishments, as they in turn recognized their own antecedents in research. But how do we rationalize the common, ubiquitous, multilateral borrowings that go on in all of scholarship--of key ideas, apt phraseology, research design, formulae, lines of argument, etc.? Is original author identification for all of these essential, advisable, ethically obligatory, or just a cognitive courtesy?

Elements and Principles

At the basal level is the idea of ideas. The new science(?) of ideonomy [see Chapter IV] demonstrates that juggling words and word lists can generate not only new syntax but new ideas. The process is an inherent characteristic of our innate symbolic skills. Pairing, tripling, etc., words of differing classes create odd and sometimes intriguing notions. Words in proximity rarely remain unperturbed. More complex than gravity, multiple semantic perturbations almost invariably result. Most may well remain nonsense phrases in the formal sense, but nonetheless have for us strange and sometimes disturbing meanings. Well, we might observe, poets do this all of the time. It is also this mechanism that can strike off new ideas and also discover "apt phrases." Using computers, the ideonomists in theory could lay claim to much of the potential content of short segments of syntax. For these technical reasons, both ideas and "apt phrases" should be exempt from the formal need of documenting and sourcing. But not exempt from the courtesy of source acknowledgement.

The sentence as an element is another matter. Sentences also form an extraordinary continuum. The standard definition that a sentence embraces a complete idea is a pedagogical ideal. I have written, I am sure, a very large number of syntactical segments that were technically sentences and contained only the vaguest of ideas. A very large number of short sentences occur in daily discourse and are therefore clearly in the public domain. The ritualistic imperative, "Have a nice day," is a recently arrived example. (Its acronym, HAND, will never catch on.)

As sentences lengthen and the word classes become less probable, uniqueness explodes. Sentences in technical, didactic, polemic journals frequently run forty, fifty, or sixty-plus words. Given the factorial nature of expanded permutations, a coherent expository sentence becomes a semantic singularity. And if valid and significant, an expository, even scholarly achievement. At this point, there is good reason to argue that source recognition becomes something more than a matter of courtesy. The term <u>propositional</u> is sometimes applied to sentences of this order, meaning that the sequence of syntax is newly invented, adaptively contrived to the communication tasks of the context involved. When valid and significant, the propositional sentence is the minimal mark of scholarship. The idea thus formulated may not be the most arresting notion of the year, but the sentence, in terms of originality, will be original to the nth degree. It will be unique.

When meaningful propositional sentences are aggregated into a well written paragraph or larger unit, then indeed has the scholar enhanced and legitimatized claims to recognition. Valid and significant scholarship cannot be anything other than original. The argument will never end over significance. Only the politics of pedagogy can resolve the relative significance of Sanskrit or software scholarship. As in contemporary mathematics that finds some infinities larger than others, propositional paragraphs are more unique than sentences.

Which is why the great "plagiarizers" are doomed to discovery. The remainder of large "borrowers" await a similar fate. Between the trivial and the great, avoiding plagiarism is the only sure route to avoid plagiarism charges. Meticulous sourcing coupled with rationalizing the concept can make the scholarly arena more humane and livable.

The epoch has passed in which footnotes, quotes, citations, and bibliographies were collectively and sometimes individually longer than the original exposition itself. Thorough scholarship had been too passionate and obsessive in documenting and crediting every semantic nuance. Credit is given not only because sound work deserves recognition and proper use creates an ethical obligation. Diligent scholarship delves the roots so that subsequent scholarship can review the fertile grounds for future intellectual efforts. Crediting sources has several purposes quite apart from maintaining academic rigor and integrity. The primary function of source citations certainly is not that of a ceremonial gesture.

Citations are supposed to be a blend of economy, practicality, and common sense. Reconciling the ethical imperative with judgment and practicality is the critical task. Not understanding the ethics and the prescribed modes can lead to disaster. Adroit citations that serve the ethics, cast in acceptable modes, and that do not impede the flow of exposition, complicate the process of composition that we have already recognized as complicated enough. Difficult choices have to be made, the purposes of the citations reviewed, and the forms of credits selected. Rarely does the scholar determine credits scaled to the validity of the materials used. Validity and significance are usually assumed. Some measure of originality is always present. Viewed synoptically, the complexities of citations are such that it would not be at all surprising that scholarship would gravitate to forms of citation that are largely pro forma and ceremonial.

Naming the author, full name, middle initial, with subsequent references to surname only begins the process. Title of source, journal or publishing house, chapter and page, paragraph and line, then resort to the traditional latinate abbreviated forms for recurring citations, such as op. cit., etc. rather quickly raises issues of frequency and form of recognition. Quoting extensive excerpts has gone out of style. One can scan dozens of pages of scholarly journals and see no quotation marks. The more common mode is a numerical superscript that is key to author and work at the point in which original concepts of others are paraphrased or otherwise employed. This is economical, but the original words of the original work have vanished. And in some instances, the originality existed only the unique verbal forms.

Style manuals can solve some of the technicalities, as can the models provided by current journals. The guidance, however, as to ethical obligations of recognizing sources is confounded by the great disparities in understanding the nature of the ethical obligation, what merits acknowledgements, and what elements of composition and in what amounts are supposed to trigger the acknowledgement process. Almost any component in any amount unacknowledged can potentially bring a charge of unfair use at the moderate end and plagiarism at the extreme.

The item of alleged plagiarism will look quite different to the original author, the user, the interested and disinterested bystander, critics, editors and ax grinders, even before the context of the usage becomes a collateral issue. Prudence has disposed neophyte writers to over cite. More experienced expositors get to know the idiom, mores, and reader expectations in acknowledgements, and they therefore can with some safety acknowledge sources more economically.

Can the basic understandings be improved? As scholarship accelerates, as it becomes more internationalized, as journals continue to multiply, producers and consumers need to review the presumptions behind acknowledgements and the assumptions generally held about the processes of exposition. Without some constraints, it can be argued that non-scholars can become pseudo scholars by adroit "borrowings" and the distinctions between legitimate and illegitimate scholarship blurred. Meticulous editing, journal refereeing, peer readings and review, and, of course, diligent, careful, thoughtful and responsive scholarship will almost invariably discover egregious cases of "borrowing."

Explicit, full attribution of all sources is impossible and not even desirable. Then what does equity in scholarship require? Attributions and recognition of significant achievements of scholarship by the most expeditious means possible. What are significant achievements? The most recent valid advances of knowledge in the area concerned: that knowledge that has not entered the general understandings of scholars or a new interpretation of what has been construed as canonical knowledge. The assumption is that genuine scholars are masters in their own fields and are recognized as such by their peers. Therefore, attributions and recognitions can be both sparse, lean, and economical.

What would happen to the scholarly enterprise if only broadly significant, demonstrably valid studies were to be published? Originality, then, would be happy by-product of the research. An unhappy by-product would that honor, recognition, tenure, and the academic good life would accrue to a much smaller minority than the current circumstance permits. The third consequence would be that academic plagiarism, when it happened, would declare itself and minor plagiarism could be easily disposed of and very likely approach a vanishing point. However, there is little probability of turning current scholarship radically toward the true and the significant.

VII

DEFINITIONS AND CONCEPTS

The world will not run short of definitions of plagiarism. Scholars and literati whip them out when the need arises and the spirit moves, almost by reflex. It follows that most definitions of plagiarism have been more or less deliberately plagiarized from earlier sources. This is the primal irony of plagiarism, but only the first of many. The typical garden variety definition is accepted without challenge. It has totally escaped critical analysis. Our notions of plagiarism consist of "received wisdom" from those who knew what they wanted the definition to do but did not care in the least how it would actually work.

Some representative definitions follow. No attempt has been made to fashion a comprehensive repository of definitions because the number of variants must run into the thousands and they are scattered everywhere: English composition texts, style manuals, term paper guidelines, college catalogues, scholarly journal manuals, legal and standard dictionaries, course syllabi, foreign publications, pedagogical literature, and texts on literary criticism. It cannot be said that the message, whatever it is, hasn't been sent. The plethora of definitions would suggest that the literary and scholarly realms are unanimous in their own minds about the reality of plagiarism whatever it is.

Authoritative sources solemnly advise us that the root meaning of the term is kidnapping. Plagiarizers were therefore abductors: abductors take things away without concern for the interests and equities of others. Literary abduction by analogy became theft and adds a further imputation of fraud by analogical extension. Analogies are acceptable forms of reasoning if the two entities actually share a reasonable number of basic features. Plagiarism as a term has bred an entire menagerie of pejorative "equivalents' recruited to the basic purpose of the definition, that is, to inhibit selectively some forms of copying.

The term _plagiarism_ has had few critics. If there are any out there, this writer has not encountered even one. In this skeptical age, finding any unexamined concept is something of a novelty. To find a sacrosanct term is almost like finding a new biological species or medical syndrome. Plagiarism shares a curious semantic feature with the term _pornography_. Even though we cannot agree on specifics, "We know it when we see it."

There are plausible reasons that a term would escape criticism. For example, no one is unhappy with it. Or it is useful and/or it works. It doesn't have to be perfect to serve its function. No one has fashioned a better one. It covers ethical, aesthetic, linguistic, and technical implications. It is comprehensive. Writers of original materials need it. No need has been found to refine it. It is too laborious to attempt to improve it. "Improvements" would make it worse. Our experience with it reveals no basic deficiencies in it. These may all be plausible, but none are logically defensible and there are no empirical reports confirming the efficacy of the term in actual operation.

Are there experts on plagiarism as there are experts on practically everything else? If one is an expert on plagiarism what does the expert know that scholars and writers generally do not? Or are all educated individuals automatically experts on plagiarism? Is plagiarism primarily a subjective matter or can it be objectified sufficiently to escape from the subjective, solipsistic trap?

Alexander Lindey and the MLA

As was noted above, Lindey prepared an entire text on plagiarism in its legal dimensions in which he recognized the classical, semantic roots of the term and offered dozens of examples in law. But he never directed critical attention to the term nor did he, based on his extensive review of case law, reach back to beneficially modify the term in the light of court decisions. His own definition was a curious hybrid showing some influences of his legal background, but he never suggested inductively modifying the definition to conform more closely to the legal realities. <u>A careful reading of Lindey leads inevitably to the conclusion that, in law, to plagiarize means taking the body of a work, the heart and core of a work, the essence of a short composition, such as melody and harmony, the unique component, and most of it. There is no formal definition current that puts such constraints on application of the term.</u>

However, Lindey's definition is a useful and proper place to start with definitions and concepts of plagiarism. "What is plagiarism?" he asks. He answers his own question thusly:

> Plagiarism is literary--or artistic, or musical--theft. It is the <u>false assumption of authorship: the wrongful act of taking the product of another's mind and presenting it as one's own.</u> Copying someone else's story, play, or song, intact, or with inconsequential changes and adding one's name to the result constitute a simple illustration of plagiarism. [Emphasis added.]

Later Lindey observes, "There can be no plagiarism without the thief's posing as the originator." And, "The essence of the wrong . . . is the appropriation of the fruits of another person's mental labor and skill."

The Modern Language Association published a definition of plagiarism in its style manual, as revised 1975, and used Lindey's definition as a point of departure. It quotes Lindey (as underlined in the above excerpt) and further stipulates:

> Plagiarism may take the form of repeating another's sentences as your own, adopting a particularly apt phrase as your own, paraphrasing someone else's argument as your own or even presenting someone else's line of thinking in the development of a thesis though it were your own. In short, to plagiarize is to give the impression that you have written or thought something that you have in fact borrowed from another. Although a writer may use other persons' words and thoughts, they must be acknowledged as such.

For a term derived from kidnapped and a definition that is supposedly drawing on Lindey's legal experience, the MLA definition extends its application of the term to phrases and thought processes as if a kidnapper could abduct portions of its victim or notions in the victim's head.

Prior to 1975, the MLA Handbook, near as determinable, did not have a formal statement on plagiarism. There can be no question that the intent of the latest (1985) revision of the statement was intended to strengthen the earlier version. Key parts are quoted below for analysis.

The present MLA concept of plagiarism is best understood by contrasting what may be copied or repeated and what may not. What is permissible: "proverbs, well-known quotations, and common knowledge." All else is proscribed. "In scholarly writing, everything derived from an outside source requires documentation--not only direct quotations and paraphrases but also information and ideas." What is meant by "derived?" Is it derived if it is already in your head as opposed to a publication in front of you? Item 5.1, What To Document, of the style manual continues, ". . . you must indicate the origin of any appropriated material that readers might otherwise mistake for your own." What specifically is meant by "appropriated material?" Copied, paraphrased, remembered? Is "common knowledge" common to the educated or the ill-informed? Who decides? Of course they mean the scholars for whom this advice has been prepared.

It takes the MLA four paragraphs in Item 1.4, <u>Plagiarism,</u> to encompass the concept and its objectives. Since the objectives are obvious, it is the concept that requires attention. Plagiarism is defined four times.

I. Plagiarism is the use of another person's ideas or expressions in your writing without acknowledging the source.

II. Simply put, plagiarism is using another person's words or ideas without appropriate acknowledgement.

III. In short, to plagiarize is to give the impression that you have written or thought something that you have in fact borrowed from someone else.

IV. . . .plagiarism is:

   a. reproducing someone else's sentences more or less verbatim, and presenting them as your own;
   b. repeating another's particularly apt phrase;
   c. paraphrasing someone else's argument;
   d. introducing another's line of thinking;
   e. failing to cite the source for a borrowed thesis.

No distinction is made between sourcing ideas and sourcing syntax. Nor does the MLA pay any serious attention to the practical consequences of such hopelessly restrictive standards on exposition. Vocabulary is entirely in the public domain, the simplest syntax, phrases, belong to us all. Short sentences, intermediate, and longer we invent and re-invent all of the time. Claims on single sentences, except for the most eloquent, would rarely be persuasive or justified. The plagiarism threshold would be more convincingly set in the neighborhood of the paragraph, where syntax, ideas and lines of thought converge, where some claim can be made to both originality and investment of intellect and an expositional core of some discernible value.

The entire version is far more stringent than that of 1975. "Repeating another's sentences" has been replaced by "another person's ideas or expressions." The emphasis remains on words <u>and</u> ideas with little reflection on the implications for scholars <u>and</u> other writers. Nor is the recurrence of "lines of thinking" and another's "arguments" helpful. For example, any intelligent, interested party can easily think of several arguments in favor or against legalizing narcotics simply because they present themselves to long term memory. It is one thing to copy such arguments verbatim out of a specific source, it is another to be denied the use of them because the original exposure to them has passed from memory.

Nor should careless over-statement exaggerate the degree of plagiarism. "The most blatant form of plagiarism is reproducing someone else's sentences, more or less verbatim, and presenting them as your own." Certainly not true. The "most blatant form" is copying an entire work, the larger and more valuable, the "more blatant."

As cited above, the MLA asserts, "everything derived from an outside source requires documentation--not only direct quotations and paraphrases, but also information and ideas." Perhaps what was meant was that everything from outside sources should be reviewed for need of documentation. It could be strongly argued that everything copied from outside sources need not necessarily be documented. If I refresh my memory from some document as to the year the U.N. came into being, must it be documented? As the paragraph suggests, "good judgment and ethics" should serve as a guide, but how will they serve documenting ideas, arguments, and lines of thought?

To plagiarize is to give the "false impression" of authorship, to mislead the reader as to authorship, or cause the reader to mistakenly assign authorship to other than the original source. However expressed, the fear is that credit will be taken for copying. The MLA obviously intends to press maximum inhibition, or perhaps it was trying to revive the anti-plagiarism fervor of earlier decades.

Definitions and Diverse Sources

From Martin and Ohmann, The Logic and Rhetoric of Exposition, Holt, Rinehart and Winston, 1963: "The academic counterpart of the bank embezzler and of the manufacturer who mislabels his product is the plagiarist, the student or scholar who leads his reader to believe that what he is reading is the original work of the writer when it is not." The authors then divide plagiarism into four species, word-for-word, the mosaic (phrase lifting), the paraphrase, and the "apt" term types. Other representative published definitions follow.

From a widely used English composition text:

> Plagiarism (from the Latin word for "kidnapper") is presenting someone else's ideas or words as your own. If you copy an article from an encyclopedia and make minor changes

> to pass it off as your writing, or if you buy someone else's term paper to hand in, you are plagiarizing deliberately. If you carelessly forget to include quotation marks or a footnote to show whose words or ideas you are using, you are plagiarizing accidentally. Whether deliberate or accidental, plagiarism is a serious offense."

From an undergraduate course catalogue and English composition class syllabus:

> The University recognizes plagiarism as a serious academic offense. Plagiarism, the act of representing the work of another as one's own, may take two forms. It may consist of copying, paraphrasing, or otherwise using the written or oral work of another without acknowledging the source, or it may consist of presenting oral or written course work prepared by another as one's own.

From Black's Law Dictionary:

> PLAGIARISM. The act of appropriating the literary composition of another, or parts or passages of his writings, or the ideas of language of the same, and passing them off as the product of one's own mind. PLAGIARIST or PLAGIARY. One who publishes the thoughts and writings of another as his own.

From the Cyclopedic Law Dictionary:

> PLAGIARISM. The act of appropriating the ideas and language of another, and passing them for one's own. When this amounts to piracy, the party who has been guilty of it will be enjoined when the original author has a copyright.

From "Plagiary", an article by Peter Shaw in the American Scholar, Summer 1982:

> At present, plagiarism is defined as the wrongful taking of and representing as one's own the ideas, words, or inventions of another.

From the Oxford English Dictionary:

> The act or practice of plagiarizing; the wrongful appropriation or purloining, and publication as one's own, of ideas, or the expression of ideas of another.

From Webster's New International:

> . . . to use without due credit the ideas, expressions, or productions of another.

From Webster's 3rd New International:

> . . . to steal or pass off as one's own (the ideas or words of another).

In a formal hearing five faculty members were asked to define plagiarism. Their verbatim responses appear below. All held doctorates, four of the five were tenured, two were full professors, and all took their academic training in representative institutions of higher learning. The professors could not agree on the lower limits of plagiarism, that is, the minimal number of words in a sequence that would require quotation marks and source identification. They all agreed that plagiarism involved both words and ideas and that misrepresentation as to authorship was the crux of the offense.

> Basically, the MLA, basically that you don't copy someone else's work and pass it off as your own. I think the definition of plagiarism is fairly precise. We normally think of plagiarism as something that is beyond reasonable. Which would be a page or a paragraph. Something that you couldn't have in your memory. Something that would be very unusual that has just crept into your work.

> The one I learned, I suppose early on in grade school, was you don't copy someone else's work. I suppose a more elegant definition would be that plagiarism consists of passing off the works of another as one's own. And subsequently I have looked up the legal definition [sic] which says that plagiarism is the appropriation of the literary composition of another and passing off as one's own the product of the mind and language of another. I think those all essentially say the same thing.

> The definition of plagiarism which I work with is one that consists of misrepresenting one's work as being completely original and not

> drawing directly from someone else's contribution. One that duplicates a contribution of exposition is as much a plagiarist as the one who duplicates ideas. . . .
>
> It would be using either words or ideas of someone without giving him credit. . . . if you take more than two, three or five words . . . you put them in quotation marks and you say right there at this point, "these are not mine. . . ."
>
> To me, plagiarism is representing as one's own work what is in fact the work of another.

These definitions could hardly be considered as tightly reasoned, cohesive and coherent. The basic assumption was that each individual scholar knew what plagiarism was and was fully competent to make formal determinations of what constitutes proper credits and plagiarism whenever called upon.

In another context, a committee of three scholars offered still another definition as an example of what it considered formal proof in plagiarism.

> If the criterion for plagiarism is whether a reader would be led to assume that the passages in question originated with the author of the paper when in fact they did not, then the specific charges were proved.

Clearly, the definitions of plagiarism, at best, are confused, and the professoriate in its interpretations, at worst, compound the confusions. Why this situation is accepted as a normal state of affairs may be something of a mystery but it is not a state of affairs that the intellectual community ought to tolerate.

A Zoology of Signs and Symptoms

Looking at the definitions in the aggregate, what are the core concepts? What do the definitions share and where do some definitions part company with others? Putting the definitions to the test should determine the relationships they bear to the concepts that they appear to embrace. Taken at their breadth and width, plagiarism straddles a plethora of continua. Whatever continuum is chosen, plagiarism extends from pole to pole. If we follow the experts, plagiarism may involve wildly diverse forms of copying:

        oral or written language
        ideas or thought
        lines of argument or thinking
        words or word sequences
        phrases or sentences, especially apt phrases
        paragraph or paragraphs
        verbatim copying or paraphrasing
        all or some copying
        wholes or parts copying
        literary or expository
        copyrighted or public domain
        conscious or unconscious
        innocent or intentional
        copying others or self
        misleading as to authorship
        inadvertent or deliberate
        careless or cunning

    These dozen and a half species probably do not exhaust the zoology of plagiarism but must comprise most of the significant forms of the pathology. From where did the expertise arise for the mastery of this plagiaristic taxonomy? On whose authority were all of the extensions made to the core notion of "using the words of others without credit?" "Oral plagiarism" is what many of us do most of the time because it is simply too laborious to assemble "references" even if we could recall them. Oral speech flows. Written exposition is teased and hammered out. Even a scholar as astute as Lindey will assert the reality of "unconscious plagiarism" and not in the least wonder how the "unconscious" soul could "pose as (the) originator" since he also says the thief must know it is theft. Otherwise, no plagiarism.

    We now know why no one has tried to formulate a comprehensive definition of plagiarism. The concept of plagiarism requires a larger and more reliable vehicle: a formula of critical criteria for determining which acts are plagiaristic and which are not. Any criteria must be intellectually defensible and of explicit practical value. And the criteria should protect legitimate rights of authors but not unreasonably inhibit the expression and exposition of others who have, or think they have, something significant to say.

The Syndrome of Plagiarism

    From the dozen and a half constraints on exposition imposed by definitions of plagiarism, some commend themselves because the courts cannot be bothered with petty verbal larceny. Others commend themselves on grounds of logic and common sense. The syndrome of plagiarism must comprise a few essential signs and symptoms that are coherent and that appear in consistent configurations. Some syndrome criteria for materials copied:

I Quality: What is copied must have significant value to the original author and the copier.

II Quantity: The crux, the core, an entity, a unified or artistic whole, must be expropriated without permission.

III Intent: There must be evidence of intent to deceive and misrepresent authorship. The evidence can be internal and textual or external and circumstantial.

IV Illicit Gain: The copier must stand to profit in some way if the deception would have been, or for a time was, successful.

V No Worthy Claim: The original work of the copier, if any, to the original work copied must be marginal or zero.

VI Printed Matter: The copying must involve written, printed, or published exposition of written, printed, or published originals.

VII Competency: The copier cannot be morally responsible if mentally or psychologically incompetent.

Yes to criteria I through VI would be flagrant and obvious, callous and deliberate, wholesale expropriation. No to competency would render the other criteria moot. No to printed matter would obviate the many possible varieties of charges of "oral plagiarism," further discussed later. In addition to the above profile, the presence or absence of extenuating and mitigating circumstances would determine the degree of plagiarism. While the function of each criterion of the profile is rather self-evident, there is no reason that it shouldn't be put to all of the tests of probable consequences that can be anticipated. Indeed, no doubt many individuals have already applied such principles in actual instances of apparent plagiarism. The root issue is the current, general approach to plagiarism and its probable outcomes in contrast to placing selective constraints on how we address the inevitable instances of copying that arise in the course of higher education.

Either we move on to a coherent notion of plagiarism or suffer what we have. If all of the elements of all of the definitions of plagiarism became bricks in a wall, we would all be walled out of the world of discourse and we would all be walled in the guilty prison of plagiarism.

Semantic Equivalents

Plagiarism, plagiarizer, plagiarist, plagiary, as terms, represent the obverse of the ethical canon of "fair use" and "proper credit." Their connotations are so bad that the mere charge of plagiarism can be and often is as devastating as plagiarism proved. The label is the academic equivalent of the mark of Cain. The synonyms that usually accompany the term plagiarism are both many and lurid: larceny, piracy, pilfering, stealing, purloining, robbery, thievery, even kleptomania. The term acts as an adhesive incendiary that spreads a poisonous mist. There is almost no end to the inventory of felonious parallels that the literary and scholarly worlds have fashioned to protect their interests.

This lexicon of loaded words is intended to inhibit the timid, intimidate the brash, and punish the perpetrators. In fact, the intellectual world has itself purloined the entire vocabulary of theft to characterize literary stealing, which is the ultimate in intellectual laziness. It is disconcerting that so little effort has been made to get behind the surface features of plagiarism.

If one espouses the theory of plagiarism as theft, then dire punishment becomes acceptable, even requisite. The very terms contain presumptions of guilt and of the kinds of guilt that far outrun the nature of the act. Explanations are not admissible and intentions of no consequence. This is very convenient for the plaintiff/accusers. The terms confuse the issue by the sheer clustering of synonyms and guilt gains by meaningless redundancy. Plagiarism and its loaded diction, ready to discharge, to wound and to maim, gain force purely because of its semantic peculiarities, singularities that can operate quite apart from the actual circumstances of citations and attributions.

Challenging the plagiarism concept itself is the verbal equivalent of engaging the Mafia. Plagiarism has spawned too many definitions, too few tenable concepts, and apparently no critics. The academy has fashioned its favorite academic abomination. Should academics be trusted to wield such an academically murderous weapon? It all started simply enough with copywork of students and scribes, a term, according to Webster, that was used to label the product of the "copyist, imitator, plagiarist, or copycat." We scribes were rebuked for failing to copy accurately but eventually were to be rebuked for the opposite offense and then admonished to "put it in your own words."

The worst that can be said of willful citation failures is that it constitutes fraud. It only remains to determine the dimensions of the fraud in the context that it occurred. Fraud, by definition, means illicit gains by illicit methods. Plagiarism is a verbal fraud. In contrast to typical notions of plagiarism, this designation is straightforward. As there are major and minor frauds, there are also major and minor plagiarisms. There is no effort here to exculpate the guilty. The intent is solely to place the analytical process on neutral grounds semantically and not permit analogical reasoning to allow guilt by metaphor. The essence of the complaint of unfair usage and deficient acknowledgement resides in the contextuals in which the offense or alleged offense occurs.

A definition is supposed to be an explicit statement of the nature of an object or idea not a loose aggregation of fragmented notions assembled by a well meaning committee. It is not fair to the camel to claim it is an animal designed by a committee. A committee is a device contrived and evolved to find the least common denominator of mental engagement. A single dedicated thinker can demolish the efforts of any but the most disciplined committees. The reader is right to ask where is the definition of this writer? Later. There are a few more considerations that may offer more focus to the concept.

VIII

CHARGES

There are important features of plagiarism charges that may not receive anything like the serious attention that they merit. The discoverers of copying may perform a quick textual analysis of pages presumed original and confirm copying from an earlier document. The experience of the discoverers is certain to trigger judgments drawn from whatever plagiarism concepts and definitions they have learned. The discoverers start as judges as well as finders. In the scholarly world there is a lot of looking and there will be, as a consequence, a lot of finding.

Charges can be made wherever and whenever anyone objects to another's copying and paraphrasing. Nor is it at all predictable as to where the charges may lead or when and how some kind of resolution occurs. Like explosives, plagiarism charges can also backfire. The charges are indifferent as to class or status. No one is immune, and some destruction is almost certain to someone, usually the one charged. The arenas rarely determine the degree of destruction, but often propel the metabolism of collateral events. The Biden Case went its supercharged course in days but its reverberations will certainly linger.

Charges in the public arena, tacit, leaked, or overt get all of the momentum the press can contrive. Charges in the scholarly press generate far less excitement. Plagiarism in scholarly journals is noted, deplored, and often quietly adjudicated. A third arena consists of charges that arouse no special attention from either public or scholarly media and go their quiet ways with only "the grapevine" intermittently passing along information concerning the parties involved. This is understandable. Usually, it is much to the advantage of the person charged not to have the charges publicly ventilated. The charges, it is understood, are damaging in themselves regardless of the objective facts that provoked them. The charging party also knows that charges can backfire and that the grapevine can be manipulated in its interest. Charges are simple, defenses complex, and outcomes often unpredictable.

Incidence

Several academic factors at work suggest that plagiarism charges are likely to increase in the college environment. It has already been noted that the MLA definition was re-written far more explicitly perhaps in intuitive appreciation of the changing scholarly environment. The earlier definition was already more than a sufficient invitation to charge.

In recent decades the college reward system has been revolutionized by notions of equity and due process. Salary increases, promotion, and tenure are now formal, documented procedures. At those institutions that adhere to scholarly productivity as a fundamental criteria for academic rewards, there will be an absolute pressure to be productive that will lead some to scholarly fraud. There is also a reverse side to the reward system that may be directed at the productive schools. The same academic due process formalities that apply to advancements also apply to dismissals and with special force to dismissal of the tenured.

There was a time that review for tenure and/or promotion was relatively uncomplicated and informal and admittedly at times even arbitrary. Faculty could decline to advance a colleague who was intemperate, an inebriate, a lecher, a crank, irascible, belligerent, tacky, or a slob. Is there anyone who has been in the groves of academe for some years who has not met them? When was the last time anyone heard of a dismissal on the above grounds? Sometimes, of course, the above miscreants were the better part of the academy. But who wants to collegiate with them? They are not now dismissible without academic grounds. As other grounds vanish, other alternatives are sought. Plagiarism is an academic ground and a very fertile one. The offense is broadly defined. Anyone who publishes is potentially at risk. The mere threat of a charge may be sufficient to separate the unloved member. The charge, when and if made, could be purely pretextual.

There would be no plagiarism and no plagiarism charges if illicit copying remained undiscovered. There are two forms of discovery: accidental and by deliberate search. Once (and only once), while listening to an informative speech by a college student on the subject of whales, the material sounded so familiar that opening a copy of the Scientific American that I happened to have with me I turned to its article on whales that I had recently read. (I don't usually carry around copies of the Scientific American.) Soon I was reading the text and hearing it word for word in a kind of plagiaristic duet. College students, undergraduates especially, have trouble with original speeches to inform because they lack or think they lack original information. The student was not challenged nor accused of plagiarism. It was observed that the material sounded as if originating from some published source. The student freely named the source but had neglected to name it in the course of the speech. In this instance, the discovery was direct and accidental. Did the student intend to deceive? Not really. The assignment called for a speech to inform and he went to a solid source of information. We discussed the need for identifying sources and giving credit to authors.

As a purely practical matter, discovery of plagiarism must occupy the high side of the probability spectrum and the more extensive the plagiarism and the more current the materials, the higher the probability. The plagiarist should be advised to find materials that are sufficiently obscure, remote and inaccessible, to escape detection. Unfortunately, such materials may also be dated, stylistically archaic, and obsolete. We may, therefore, safely conclude that the incidence of plagiarism will continue at least about the same as in the past.

As long as discovery continues, the discoverers will be tempted to make charges. In one respect the charge of plagiarism is a marvelous one to make. Someone, somewhere will find any source dependency in any degree to be plagiarism. More than that, it does not take a vigorous hunt to find a definition that will fit the alleged offense.

In written exposition of students (and not students alone) the troublesome impression periodically arises that the materials are somewhat or even rather familiar. Much academic exposition is stylistically sterile. Personality is deliberately excluded, presumably in the pursuit of objectivity. Part of our remarkable human decoding abilities is that of pattern detection, but, of course, that's about all reading is apart from the semantic stirrings that it is supposed to accomplish. The student's native style and idiom is quite unlike the rather formal exposition of professional writers. Again, the student's insertions and adaptations contrast sharply with the original text. So while college presidents engage ghost writers, college students are not supposed to submit ghosted term papers.

Oral plagiarism tends to be self-incriminating whether the materials are memorized or read from the printed page. Oral reading is a minor fine art, in that the printed page is difficult to convert to something analogous to living speech. It requires the best efforts of actors to make printed communication resemble spontaneous speech. The printed medium tends to retain its lexical identity. The style of exposition is unlikely to correspond to the oral style of the speaker. The listener would know when and where the speaker would dip in and out of his own idiom in those instances in which the speaker made strategic adaptations in the materials. To confirm the discovered copying, the first place to look was in an easily accessible usable source that often turned out to be the **Reader's Digest**. Even its sometimes casual style was not usually convertible to conversational style of live speech. There were some instances in which it was obvious that the materials were copied but short of a full time detective agency, some sources of original matter would be difficult to locate.

In an instance involving faculty, a professor claimed an equity in a corporate document prepared by a special commission. The subject matter and the treatment of it set off the pattern matching warning bell way back somewhere in consciousness. A quick examination of the files turning up a virtually identical document dated three years earlier than the vita enhancing document recently submitted. The professor had no claim whatsoever on the document. Claim of authorship was withdrawn. No disciplinary action was taken. The materials were technically in the public domain, but on no account should spurious authorship be claimed.

The Impact of Charges

Given the rhetorical stigma of the term itself, the charge of plagiarism will punish the accused whether the alleged offense is adjudicated or not. The one charged is doomed to live under the dark cloud of intellectual dishonesty that no subsequent exoneration can every fully dissipate. The charges are supercharged and are remembered. What the public charges do not accomplish, the grapevine will complete. The defenses are laborious and easily overlooked and forgotten. These realities alone should induce the scholarly community to heed the admonition of Alexander Lindey: ". . . there is too much plagiarism crying." Too much or too little in the academy, the scholarly community has no excuse for being ill-informed about the realities of exposition and acknowledgements.

The presumption favors the scholar who brings the charges. What conscientious scholar would launch charges without credible evidence? The problem may be that the evidence is only credible but not demonstrable or provable. In the minds of spectators, a plagiarism charge becomes its own judge and jury. The presumption is that of guilt because the charging party or group is often assumed to be more dedicated to scholarship, sensitive and ethical than the individual targeted by the charge.

Plagiarism charges in the academic community are considered so serious that the American Association of University Professors (AAUP) published an advisory letter on the subject, <u>Letter 15, A Charge of Plagiarism, AAUP Bulletin, 51:71, Spring 1975.</u> As the advisory letter notes, charges of plagiarism are doubly serious in that both the individuals involved on either side and the institution risk reputations whether the charges are valid or not. The advisory letter recommended resort to external, expert, independent agencies for determination of procedures and standards to be used in adjudicating cases. Knowing the sheer devastation that charges can cause, the prejudicial climate that charges create, and the technical incompetence of scholars in judging plagiarism, the argument for objective, expert assessment is overwhelming.

There is a common contention that a person charged is innocent until proven guilty. But the individual charged with plagiarism frequently is obliged to demonstrate innocence by proving the negative side of the case. This is not a practical tactic because some "expert" on plagiarism will affirm that there is a species of plagiarism done in innocence. The alleged expert will ignore the contradictions to which casual definitions of plagiarism lead. The burden of proof traditionally must be carried by the prosecutor on behalf of the plaintiff. Instead, the defendant is challenged to prove that what was done was not some form or another of plagiarism. Give the MLA definition of plagiarism a careful reading, and if you have written much, how confidently will you defend yourself to each and every one of its stipulations? Or perhaps the MLA definition doesn't mean what it says and it is only an admonitory metaphor, a well meant guide to exposition. That is not the way it has been used nor the way it will be used.

The AAUP *Letter 15* is rightly concerned about institutional reputation. There are collateral consequences equally grave. Charges polarize the parties. The contest will be everything an academic inquiry should not be: total war, hardened positions, a contest of wills, cunningness, deviousness, ruthless and mean, ending finally in a monomania of academic kill or be killed. The charges will require mobilizing support in favor and against. There will not likely be any neutrals, yet neutrality and objectivity is an absolute requirement of justice.

Investigation

A proper investigation must precede charges and the ramification of charges understood as the investigation proceeds. To preserve the presumption of innocence the investigation should be completely confidential and with the knowledge of the individual under investigation. The one investigated would err gravely to prefer a public review at the start, especially if the investigators are third party "experts" totally detached from the political arena of the investigation. It is in the interests of both the institution and the charged party to have an independent assessment of the charges. It is in the interests of the chargers to have the task done by locals particularly if the charges are possibly pretextual because the contest will be more political than intellectual.

The object of the initial investigation is to determine the species and degrees of copying that warranted investigation in the first place. It is in the interest of all parties, except those with hidden agendas, to move toward charges in full command of all aspects of the case if the evidence leaves no alternative but to file formal charges. A meticulous, objective case that meets basic standards should result in a quiet resignation and should never go to court. Anything less will be a multilateral embarrassment and will invite protracted, exhausting, internal conflict with the courts called in to settle business that is properly that of the institution.

The Grounds for Charges

Positive Criteria

I. INTENT: There must be evidence of intent to deceive and to misrepresent authorship. The burden of proof must be on the accusers.

II. GAIN: The copier must stand to profit illicitly in some significant way by the act assuming the fraud's success.

III. COPYING: The copier must expropriate materials in quality and/or quantity that comprise a core, an expositional entity, a unified conceptual or artistic whole. Plagiarism involves length as well as depth. The degree of the offense is proportional to the value of the materials copied.

Negative Criteria

I. INCOMPETENCY: A copier, however diligent, cannot be held responsible if psychologically or mentally incompetent. Emotional disorders are not unheard of in the academy. Those ignorant of the rules by accidents of language, culture, or educational deficiencies are candidates for re-education, not punishment. A semi-literate star athlete who copies under academic stress indicts the school not himself.

II. ACKNOWLEDGE-
MENTS: Any evidence pointing to the original author or source mitigates the intent to deceive even if source identification is textually distant from the materials copied or is less than adequate on other grounds. Deliberate manuscript changes obviously designed to obscure recognition of original author clearly strengthen the case in favor of the charges.

III. ADDENDUM: Did the copier add anything of substance to the materials copied? Plagiarism is mitigated if some original work finds its way into that which was copied. For a sound contribution, for good and great recastings of prior original expositions, we have traditionally excused the great copiers. If the copier has any worthy claim on the aggregate result, to that extent, the primary offense of copying is mitigated. Not entirely forgiven, just mitigated.

In addition to the above, there are threshold criteria. The copying of "apt phrases" should not lead to charges and there isn't much evidence that they do. Apt phrases wear out quickly by excessive oral use as well as written repetition. *Idea* plagiarism is a fruitless pursuit. All ideas are nested in other ideas and so are implicit in other ideas. Persistent, excessive copying of individual sentences and separate paragraphs could merit initial investigation but the investigators should look carefully at Positive Criteria III above.

Evidence of all three positive criteria is required for formal charges. Evidence of incompetency is an absolute mitigating circumstance. Punishing the incompetent is both vengeful and arbitrary. The other two mitigating and extenuating circumstances, if present to a significant degree, could easily make formal charges questionable even in the presence of evidence of some degree of intent to deceive, of undocumented copyings and illicit gain. But all must receive thorough consideration prior to formal action.

IX

COPYING PRACTICES AND EXAMPLES

The purpose of this section is to examine copying practices and examples in the context of the traditional definitions and the definition of verbal fraud advanced in the Epilogue. Having advanced a concept it is only fair to see how it works out in practice. There is no way to gain a synoptic vision of the universe of scholarly exposition to see whether contemporary modes of scholarly attributions are responding to new needs and perceptions. Certainly the behavioral evidence suggests an increasing degree of casualness in sourcing modes. One established scholar, who responded to some inquiries regarding alleged plagiarism, made the following observations by letter with no expressed constraints on its use in any contexts. It is highly instructive.

> With original papers the serious question is whether or not the claimed new <u>results</u> have been copied from someone else. However, the material presented in setting up the question or the method of solution or analysis is usually taken from previously published work and often only with a vague reference. It disturbs the flow of a paper to try to attribute every phrase or formula to its source and most of the profession would, I believe, find it perfectly acceptable to use the common practice of using publicly available sections of research papers, provided no claim to originality is made for this section, and that a general reference is given. If someone else has found a particularly good way of phrasing a question this soon becomes part of common practice and is even not attributed eventually in the literature.
>
> Survey papers, with no claim to originality, of necessity summarize other material, and when writing them it is usual to use actual phrases from other works. There is no standard practice about giving detailed references, for large sections copied from elsewhere attribution is usual, but for smaller sections and formulas not necessarily so, provided a general reference to the work is included somewhere in the relevant section. Papers that are too meticulous in attribution become unreadable and editors will ask for a re-write.

Textbooks are more difficult to discuss, as practice varies widely. Virtually all textbooks copy to some extent, the obvious case being the use of end-of-chapter examples.

Turning now to his work, the paper I can comment on most confidently is the first paper--on housing starts--which quotes my own work. I found his use of sections of my work with only general attribution to be completely common practice.

Since the alleged plagiarist admitted using verbatim paragraphs, albeit with source attributions, no textual analysis is necessary. The essential point clearly stressed in the first quote above was whether new research findings were copied and claimed as original work. Using this criterion the accused was not by either intent or practice guilty of plagiarism or any species of verbal fraud.

In another context is a document used in defense of a plagiarism charge that demonstrates by example the academic community's attribution practices. Only representative samples are needed for analysis although the copying modes modified as the document became more extended. The document, without end matter, consisted of fifty-three double-spaced typewritten pages. It was characterized as a draft.

A single page, three paragraph introduction contains two self-references to "this paper" suggesting it to be a distinctive and original document. But the first paragraph of the first of eight sections identifies the materials as a rewrite. The copier or the copier's agent(s) had assembled several basic sources on the subject and settled on three major useful sources. The splicings and strategic deletions and insertions was obviously laborious work. Thence, the mode of copying shifted to major expropriations with only minor adaptations.

Original Text:
Copied Portions Underlined

Given the conflicting pressures exerted by these multiple constituencies, the president feels that he <u>alone</u>, with the assistance of the officers of the central administration, <u>can make the compromises, adjustments, and accommodations necessary to accomplish the overall institutional goals of the university. Discussion, consultation, and debate may be helpful</u>--faculty <u>advisory bodies do have a</u>

role--but the authority and responsibility for final decisions must always rest with the central administration.

Thus the hierarchical model is not uncongenial to the administration. Furthermore, the faculty does not necessarily object. Many professors are perfectly content to let the administration--the "money men"--worry about funding the university so long as the faculty are left free to pursue their teaching and research. The typical professor is concerned not with where the money comes from, but with getting his share of it. A professor's loyalty, if any, is not so much to his institution as to his profession. In the final analysis, the professor does not identify with the university as an organization whose survival, development, and growth have a significant effect on his or her personal success as a scholar, but rather regards it as little more than a convenient, and possibly transient, infrastructure for professional pursuits.

Paraphrased Version

There is not a single academic institution in this country where debates over money are not as central as those over programs and purpose. Recently faculty and staff have recognized that debates over budgets and allocations are also debates over campus power and institutional goals. In these debates, administrators have had the upper hand. They understood the intricacies of the management and budget process while faculty and staff generally did not. Conversely, the typical professor has not been concerned with where the money comes from but with getting his share of it. A scholar's loyalty has often been not so much to his institution as to his profession. The professor may not identify with the university as an organization whose survival, development, and growth has a significant effect on his or her personal success as a scholar, but rather may regard it as a convenient, and possibly transient, vehicle for professional pursuits.

> In this situation, university administrators may feel that they <u>alone can make the compromises, adjustments, and accommodations necessary to accomplish the overall institutional goals of the university</u>, particularly when faced with externally imposed constraints. <u>Discussion, consultation, and debate may be helpful--collegial advisory bodies do have a role</u>--but statutory <u>authority and responsibility for final decisions</u> has remained <u>with the central administration</u>.

The copier(s) subsequently used verbatim, with negligible modifications, sequences of "assumptions" about the subject, formats followed in the subjects' procedures and even an entire glossary pertinent to the subject all without quotation marks, citation numbers or any author identification within the text. The only mitigating circumstance was that the three sources from which the more than forty pages were copied did appear in the appended nine item bibliography. The materials copied were copyrighted standard expository materials on the subject, authoritative, representative and reasonably thorough on a complex, controversial subject. The rewrites interpolated between the copyings, totaling perhaps seven to eight double-spaced typewritten pages added little or nothing to the merit of the originals except for shaping the whole into an apparently original tract. The purpose of the document seemingly was to demonstrate that the administrator who promulgated it was in full command of the subject and prepared to react appropriately when circumstances warranted. The extensive uncredited copying, clear infringement of copyright, far beyond any acceptable degrees of fair use, was by a scholar/professor and specifically directed to the attention of the academic community. All traditional canons of plagiarism were met.

These were very prosaic, general knowledge commonplaces about the subject concerned. In equity the materials merited much better source recognition than received. Original research was not involved. Although widely disseminated, no one cried plagiarism. Apparently there was a tacit assumption that such expository materials were in the public domain and the rather obvious "dependency" on prior original documents a minor matter, similar to the views expressed in the letter quoted above. Should the perpetrator(s) experience rebuke, reprimand, reminders, remediation, condemnation? Is this a solid case of verbal fraud, largely unrelieved by extenuating and mitigating circumstances justifying severe punishment or even career destruction? It is tempting to cry foul and demand fitting retribution. The fact was that no one complained although the document was rather clear evidence that plagiarism standards in the academy shouldn't be taken too seriously.

Regarding the episode noted earlier, page 4, the curious reader can consult the <u>Point of View</u> pages of the <u>Higher Educational Chronicle</u>, May 7, 1979 and May 20, 1987 for complete texts of the original version and the rescript that triggered its readers to contextual comparisons. There is a lesson here for those tempted to do copywork. The highly patterned printed word imprints long term memory rather well. The excerpt below represents the most grievous sample of verbatim usage of the whole although the use made of the original also included elements of format, major and minor ideas, general theme and tonality.

Original

FREEDOM--Despite pressures of college work, you've had freedom you'll never have again.
> Freedom of daily schedule will be sorely missed--no more naps, tennis, TV, checking mailbox for tenth time--henceforth daylight hours will be spent indoors.
> Freedom of holidays gone also--no more half-week Thanksgivings, two-week Christmases, summer off. Now Thanksgiving is Thursday, Christmas the 25th, summer just like the rest of the year.
> Freedom of choice. Also--you've chosen courses, instructors, schedules, even colleges; chosen topics of interest within courses; chosen activities out of class. Starting now freedom is sacrificed to will of the corporation.

TEMPORARINESS--College is like Monopoly game--fold up board and forget about bankruptcies and shattered hopes.
> In college, repeat a course if fail; do poorly and shrug it off; cut class if oversleep; miss one question but get the next; get note from doctor and be excused from anything; flunk out of one college, go somewhere else.
> All the great challenges of last four years were only games--if you fail to meet them, no big deal; easy come, easy go; fold up Monopoly board, all problems vanish; start new game anytime.

Rescript

Despite the pressures of college work, you had freedom such as you will never have again. You could arrange your own daily schedule. In the future there will be no more naps, tennis, or hoops at 3 p.m. and no more daytime television. The majority of your daylight hours from now on will be spent indoors working. Your holiday freedom is also over--no more half-week Thanksgiving, Christmas will be December 25, and summer will be just like the rest of the year. You will look forward to two-week vacations and, after 20 years, the possibility that you will get a month off. If you plan to be self-employed, kiss all vacations goodbye for the first 10 years.

Until now you also had an unprecedented freedom of choice. You had the opportunity to choose instructors and courses and your own activities outside of class. In the future, you will have to barter for much of that freedom with the benefactor who pays your salary or that of your clients.

College was not unlike a Monopoly game. At any time, you could fold up the board, forget about bankruptcies and bad investments, and start over.

There is an opportunity for students of expository writing to compare the format and text of the original prepared by a self-identified "head of . . . writing program" at Rutgers with the rescript by a Professor of Chemistry, the University of Wisconsin at Eau Claire. Forgetting the primary audience, presumably students who assiduously read the Chronicle, after several readings this reader preferred the rescript version that also included some development of a few basic ideas. Was enough added to make any claim on the original? The problem is that the original version can be considered original only in general format and in specific language formulations. Commencement addresses, pseudo or not, are rarely examples of original exposition. Those who have suffered through decades of annual commencement addresses are always mentally writing alternative versions as speakers strive and usually fail to meet the ceremonial obligations of being stimulating and energizing. It is an almost impossible rhetorical task that can be met gracefully at best; grace and wit. Both versions come up short, yet purport to be saying novel truths to the departing undergraduates. We academics have all heard better and worse. The Chronicle was wise in not labeling the copying plagiarism, a term best reserved for those species of copying that embody not only intent but the illicit use of materials of intrinsic value.

Under MLA definitions and all standard published definitions, the examples and practices above and all of the other instances cited in this monograph, are species of some degree of plagiarism. The same examples simultaneously demonstrate that such copyings are commonplace occurences, and that the academic community is, in fact, frequently complacent about plagiarism and then quixotically and intermittently hysterical about plagiarism. A most curious state of affairs. Scholars laud equity and worship intellectual consistency. But not in the realm of copying.

CHAPTER X

THE BIDEN CASE

Senator Biden's fall from political grace is a perfect demonstration of how lethal plagiarism charges can be. The New York Times in a front page story September 12, 1987 inferred that the senator had engaged in oral plagiarism of a campaign commercial that had British Labor Party candidate Neil Kinnock waxing eloquent. (But not eloquent enough apparently. He lost to Margaret Thatcher.) The senator made the mistake of slavishly following the model, using phraseology, ideation, mini-scenes and plot, partly perhaps because of some parallelism in their experiences and commonality of rhetorical style. In twelve days the slip turned into an avalanche and a credible presidential candidacy was crushed.

The scene, according to the news releases, was the senator's closing speech at an Iowa State Fair debate, August 23. Debates are supposed to be fully documented and the content otherwise original with the debater. Not so usually, with what now passes for political debates. The news release reported the senator as having begun his remarks by saying the ideas had "come to him spontaneously on the way to the debate."

What ideas? Kinnock's main theme, i.e., "Why am I the first Kinnock in a thousand generations to be able to get to (sic) university?" Kinnock then included his wife in the "thousand generations" rhetorical figure. Senator Biden, apparently entranced by this rhetorical flourish, used the same dual gambit in his Iowa debate without credit and had compounded his copying by claiming the thought came to him "spontaneously."

The story first appeared in the New York Times, date line September 11, 1987, and received full TV coverage September 12. The excerpt below is from the St. Louis Post-Dispatch, September 13:

> In his closing speech at a debate at the Iowa State Fair on Aug. 23, Biden lifted Kinnock's closing speech from the commercial without crediting him, the newspaper said.
>
> In the commercial, Kinnock begins: "Why am I the first Kinnock in a thousand generations to be able to get to university?" He then points to his wife in the audience and continues: "Why is Glenys the first woman in her family in a thousand generations to be able to get to

university? Was it because all our predecessors were thick?"

Biden began his remarks, the *Times* said, by saying the ideas had come to him spontaneously on the way to the debate.

"I was thinking as I was coming over here, why is it that Joe Biden is the first in his family ever to go to a university?" he said. Then, pointing to his wife, he continued: "Why is it that my wife who is sitting out there in the audience is the first in her family to ever go to college? Is it because our fathers and mothers were not bright? Is it because I'm the first Biden in a thousand generations to get a college and a graduate degree that I was smarter than the rest?"

Other parts of both speeches were very close in their tone and content. Biden's aides and the candidate was traveling and did not care to comment.

The Kinnock Paraphrase

Why these phrases so untimely uttered? It must have seemed meaningful and irresistible at the time, but what was intended by the "thousand generations" phrase? At twenty years per generation, the Kinnocks and the Bidens have been waiting for college admission since about 18,000 BC! They would have had to matriculate in Alley Oop Institute or Neanderthal U. Then Kinnock asks, "Was it because all of our predecessors were thick?" Biden follows the cue but modifies the question, "Is it because . . . I was smarter than the rest?" Is this once again the old "humble origins but look at me now" ploy? These are purely rhetorical questions if there ever were any, certainly not to be taken seriously. What Biden chose to rescript was frivolous, even silly. He raised the question of his intelligence at the very moment he was demonstrating a lack of it. Biden purloined piffle. And poorly timed piffle just prior to the opening of his big opportunity as presidential candidate to flex his political and moral powers to defeat the appointment of Judge Bork to the Supreme Court.

The *Times* article quotes Senator Biden as saying, "I don't like this stuff you've written for me." One of his advisors is quoted as saying, "He (Biden) didn't even know what he said. He was just on automatic pilot." So Kinnock inadvertently provided Biden with a ghost written close to a U.S. presidential candidate's debate, who behaved in a manner reminiscent of the behavior criticized in Ronald Reagan, that is, he doesn't know what he is talking about.

The content, supposedly, was to demonstrate the power government has to expand horizons, challenge the mind and open opportunities previously denied to some. A most legitimate subject for political oratory as long as political passion doesn't burst into hyperbole. As facts and reality should never be ignored, gross overstatement is still to be deplored.

It is typical of plagiarism charges that often the significance of <u>what</u> was used is totally ignored in favor of the fact that it <u>was</u> used. Not much content analysis will be wasted on Biden's paraphrasing. The paraphrastic pattern was there and that was all that was needed. He not only tended habitually to paraphrase, the Kinnock episode quickly led to his past use of uncredited text in a paper done as a law student. Failed for plagiarism! That revelation crystalized the pattern. Then the senator, under duress, panicked and the whole episode went out of control. Rather simple, paraphrastic habits infused and ignited the context so that the initial charge of plagiarism became, as it is said in law, pretextual. The real issue became the man and not the act.

The Context

The candidate created only part of the context of charges and review. It is where the context that he created met the context of the current climate of the public arena that did him in, especially as it was shaped by the press. The modest paraphrasing caused the candidate to be at turns, defensive, accusative, boastful, assertive, apologetic, inaccurate, and erroneous at the core of the issue; the evidence of his honesty and integrity, based on his record. His posture, as they say, was orator, scholar, intellect, idealist. His behavior was anger, indignation, brittleness, and shifty. Others were responsible for his predicament: the press, supporters, competitors, and adversaries. The senator was the obverse of "grace under pressure." The key, perhaps, was in his concern for perceptions of his intelligence. As with Kinnock, there was some question of his claim to education, to office, and by extension the very powers he was now exercising. He was too intelligent to have intended to deceive. Which he was. But the record was otherwise. It did not endorse his intelligence and neither did his behaviors.

It was Senator Biden's terrible misfortune that his minor slip followed Senator Hart's incomprehensible behavior. And that both quick-minded senators did not realize they were walking the shadows cast by revelations of the foibles and/or philanderings of Roosevelt and Eisenhower, the Kennedys, Nixon before and during Watergate, the duplicities of the Iran-Contra scandal, and the peccable evangelicals. Scandals and disgrace power the presses. Long running battles and skirmishes among the notables keep controversies and issues alive. Something odd has happened. Ethics, it might seem has gathered some momentum. Well, maybe.

A reminder is in order of what the press is and is not. Its function is to make money as the function of politics is to wield power which is only coin of a different realm. The press is not, therefore, an agency of information, providing an objective array of representative facts, nor offering careful, thoughtful, neutral, balanced analysis, except in the most exceptional cases. Usually both content and opinion is shaped or bent to the purpose of publication or broadcast and contains the preconceptions most consonant with that purpose. Without money, they wouldn't publish. With it, there is no escaping a conflict of interest. It is an unresolvable dilemma. Yet the press is far safer with money as its master than government.

Defensive Defense

Plagiarism occasionally is indefensible but is usually defensible on some grounds. A few of the senator's supporters and some commentators resorted to the "everyone does it" defense mode that might have worked if there had been but a single episode. A campaign aide noted that the Kinnock paraphrase had been used twenty-five to thirty times with inadvertent omission of attributions only a few times, including the atypical Iowa instance. A thoughtful few pointed out the commonality of ideas and their varied if similar syntactical garb: where Roosevelt, Kennedy, Churchill, even Lincoln had deliberately or inadvertently used memorable syntax that demonstrably had been used in the past, sometimes virtually verbatim or with very close paraphrases. Which is really all that the Kinnock rescript amounted to. The pattern of the press is to look around for patterns, with Hart, Biden, Reagan, or anyone else. When the law school uncredited copying turned up, the senator wanted the public to know that he didn't copy because he lacked intelligence and he strove to demonstrate his intelligence by directing attention to his academic record as, coincidently, we might think, Hart challenged the press to find a philandering pattern in his behavior. From both of those turning points the media made and manipulated the news. Events overwhelmed both.

Those charged with plagiarism frequently do not have the luxury of allies. Despite pious assurances from various quarters, the person charged is truly a lonely figure. The senator's candidacy folded fast because his financial backers immediately wondered what other surprises lie ahead. And they must have covertly resented their former candidate's lack of early candor. But how could candidate Biden, running for any office, say in passing, "Oh, by the way, I flunked a course for plagiarism at law school." It is not the kind of thing that ordinary prudent humans put in their credentials. Without backers, the battle for the candidacy was over. The battle to restore his integrity lies ahead, and unless the senator manages that contest carefully, his political career will be in jeopardy.

There is no question that Senator Biden is very bright, but he himself has raised the question of his wisdom and poise. He will require resiliency and reconstruction of his claim to honesty and integrity. He cannot complain that he was held to standards largely ignored by others even though it is true. He has suffered no real losses just that of an opportunity, and not the kind that would interest the EEOC. If he were black or female, he could claim conspiracy, unequal treatment, and discrimination. All would be true. But there is no constituency for members of the white male minority. It is a fair but fundamentally unanswerable question: would his candidacy have failed as quickly, or at all, if he had been female or black? Jesse Jackson got away with a racist, ethnic slur when he referred to New York City as "Hymie town." That insensitive reference would have destroyed any gentile politician who might have made the same slip. Plagiarism is also a matter of discriminations made and not made.

The defense against plagiarism charges is almost always slow and laborious. Senator Biden was allowed little time and badly used the time he had. Recovery from plagiarism is almost invariably a painfully slow process. Rehabilitating the senator will be a challenging task to be handled with extreme care. The best guess would be that the damage is permanent. Plagiarism casts a long and dark shadow.

Biden and Ethics

Aristotle observed that ethical proof is crafted by careful, meticulous, equitable, even-handed behaviors, laboriously earned, easily destroyed. Aristotle illuminated integrity and honor. It is fairly safe to say that he would have had nothing but contempt for images, posturing, and credibility. There will be an avalanche of commentary on the meaning of the Biden political debacle. Everyone will have heart-felt advice for the senator on how to recapture the affections of the public and put his political ambitions back on track. Also, these pundits of diverse persuasion will all incontrovertibly know what the public is looking for as the senator reconstitutes his behaviors.

The senator has already indicated his intention to do better, has apologized, and indicated his inclination to return to presidential politics in the future. Unfortunately, his explanation that defeating Judge Bork's nomination was more important than his own presidential aspirations was pure rationalization in the face of confronting realities. The plagiarism charges had left him defenseless, his backers in wonderment. His chairmanship and senator's seat were all that he had left. His constituency will continue to love him if he defeats Bork. But the Bork supporters will never forgive and forget. Politicians also have very long memories. So do judges. What if Bork manages to win? What if Senator Biden tries to practice law in Bork's court?

No one has accused the U.S. Senate of being a seat or font of ethics. The chair that Senator Biden holds, the Senate allows him manipulate to defeat a proposition before that body. It is the right of the Senate to play the game its own way. But as a parliamentary matter, chairs are supposed by their experience, judgment and wisdom, to guide their deliberative bodies to the best conceivable, rational consensus. Chairs are not supposed to steer parliamentary bodies in the direction of chairs' forgone conclusions. Yet Senator Biden announced his intention to oppose Bork before the hearings started. On several grounds, Senator Biden would have been wiser to relinquish the chair, or at least announce his redoubled intention to give Justice Bork all possible considerations of equity (<u>without</u> mentioning that he himself had not been the beneficiary of such consideration in the recent past). The absence of both solicitude and objectivity given the bizarre circumstances suggests the presence of much deeper motivations.

So what ethics might the public expect? Reality is always apparently simple and deceptively subtle. They are looking for integrity. A person who has or projects wholeness. Modern political landslides are made from the personal integral qualities of Roosevelt, Eisenhower, Reagan, Truman (whose election was a counter-landslide), and perhaps John Kennedy, had he survived long enough for re-election. Poised, self-confident, open, good humored, responsive. What of integrity? All had it or projected it. Reagan survived the Iran-Contra scandal. Expectations are not the same for office holders and office seekers. The jury is out on philandering. But not on denying it in the presence of circumstantial or direct contrary evidence. Such behavior is not the response of persons of integrity.

The public is not looking for a compulsive truth teller. It is looking for a judicious use of the truth. The art of lying should not be wasted on trivia. The public expects discretionary lying in the nation's interest unless it gets too blatant and its purposes and consequences are questionable as in the Iran-Contra hearings. In a dangerous, deceitful world, deception is not only frequently necessary, it is occasionally even admirable. The essence of honesty is not to lie about lying. Do we deny we use "white lies?" Then we are concerned. When we are obviously caught in a lie, then denial is a lie to save a lie and merely foolish. Integrity cannot tolerate habitual lying because functional, social interactions become impossible and the habitual liar is socially or politically useless. If plagiarism misrepresents, then another related misrepresentation is where integrity quickly begins to disintegrate.

Post Mortem I

The public doesn't care about attributions, image or credibility, and at best knows that plagiarism is a bad word. It sounds bad and it's associated with words, i.e., words that come to plague you. For Senator Biden, it was verbal plague. He is now a case. All remaining presidential candidates are on notice and will receive equal time, media energy, and attention. As the French Revolution demonstrated, once the guillotine is rolling it is hard to stop it. Once unfair, it is only fair to be unfair again. All other candidates were invited to comment on the departure of Senator Biden from the race. All successfully suppressed their secret delight at his departure, but only in the grim realization that each would experience a search that would at least rival the scrutiny given Judge Bork and Joe Biden. Is it likely that remaining candidates and candidates yet to be are all "slipless?" Exactly who snitched on Biden? Who supplied the tapes and transcripts? How was it done? Should it have been done? Do we really know why it was done except for obvious motivations? Will it all come out, or are there forces at work that can erase the trail?

Can Joseph Biden rise from the politically dead following the sobering example of the resurrections of Richard Nixon? Could the charge of plagiarism have the same lethal effect as the fact of Chappaquidick had on Senator Kennedy's presidential aspirations? If it does, then a plagiarism charge is a kiss of death to character, especially painful in that Senator Biden "borrowed" little and what little he copied was material of no substantial value.

Post Mortem II

Human affairs consist of agendas, and agendas within agendas. To all events there are surface features and deep features. As noted earlier, language not only can treat of the apparent and the real, but is also similarly applied. Is that all there is to the Biden case? Not likely! What is most instructive is what is left unsaid. As yet commentators and opinion makers have used their intellects only as surface vehicles. If they do delve what are they likely to find? A far more probable scenario and a plot that would charm Arthur Conan Doyle. There is both a Biden case and a Biden story.

Many years ago a very bright but not very meticulous law student was required to prepare a paper as a course assignment.

Assembling materials in preparation, some writings were so lucidly appropriate and conclusive to the paper's purpose they simply fell into place and the student's innate and strong syntactical skills didn't notice the transition. In went the paper. It was not returned with a grade indicative of academic merit as was expected. Instead, he was summoned before a mini-tribunal to explain his uncredited verbatim usages. He was thunderstruck, crushed. His career hopes, his ambitions "trembled in the balance." Everyone knew that a frequent punishment for plagiarism was expulsion. But his record suggested it was a first offense. His punishment would be emphatic but mitigated. A reprimand, failure in the course, and the course to be repeated. A terrible trauma. Would he ever forget it? Never! The incident recedes into the past. Events unfold. His destiny is being reshaped. He becomes a United States senator from Delaware. He had no way of knowing that he was enroute from trauma number one to trauma number two. The plot was thickening.

In an off-year election, the Republicans lose majority control of the Senate. A rising, relatively young political star is awarded the chairmanship of the judiciary committee. His qualifications: seniority, oratory, and presidential ambitions. The magnificent irony could not have but amused him. He, an indifferent student of the law, would now lay it down for others with high legal ambitions. Then the President, incomprehensibly, forwarded the name of a most prolific, prodigious, politically vulnerable legal scholar as candidate for the Supreme Court! Oh, joy supreme! The mediocre student of law could demonstrate his comparable intellectual skills before the entire nation and by using the powers of his chairmanship keep a conservative intellect off the court.

Triply delicious: an enormous boost to his presidential ambitions, solidifying his liberal, civil rights oriented constituencies and the ultimate revenge on all who questioned his intellectual powers. Did the senator not think of these things? Of course he did! A final and fit balm for his terrible trauma of yesteryear. He could not conceal his euphoria as he assumed the judiciary chair. He announced he would use it to defeat Justice Bork. He would be fair, of course, even as he was busy mobilizing the vociferous opposition.

Who sets the climate of the hearings as opposed to the passions excited by proponents and opponents? The presiding chair! He permitted haranguing, haggling, preposterous opinions--it wasn't a deliberative hearing at all and was never intended to be. Justice Bork was treated as a criminal in the dock, presumed guilty. Numerous witnesses were paraded by to testify to his brutal callousness, intellectual duplicity, mainstream humanity, his civil rights "insensitivity," his judicial restraint, his legal scholarship, the split personality of Robert Bork. And in the middle of this feast, like a picnic thunderclap, the senator was jolted by Trauma Two.

Biden and Bork

For politicians, delving into comparative ethics is a losing game. It was, by some, considered just routine business to pull the plug on Biden. The plug pullers knew that the copying offense was insignificant and the impact of charges lethal. They knew that once revealed the chant of plagiarism would be magnified and irradiated into the public consciousness. Like a pin pricking a balloon, a negligible cause had a catastrophic effect. The object was to destroy on totally insubstantial grounds. The disparity between ends and means is often the slough of unethical behavior. The Dukakis campaign managers found mean-spiritied means to atrocious political ends. Biden was not fair game nor given a sporting chance. But what did Biden do for Bork?

It should be said that neither side in the Bork hearings distinguished themselves any more than did the candidate. The nomination of Robert Bork to the Supreme Court was handled by the administration with about as much adroitness as it handled the Iran-Contra affair. Bork, the legal scholar, was on the slab ready for autopsy. Bork, the legal scholar, addressed all questions directed to him with the halo of his cap and gown illuminating his rhetorical legalese. His majority adversaries and minority supporters simply counted the deliverable votes of their constituencies and rendered a political verdict. Bork lost.

Bork was described by most as a man of honor but little understanding. The Supreme Court is the legal pinnacle and ambition sometimes must suffer to ascend such a peak. But Bork tolerated a kindless, merciless grilling that no man of honor would likely endure. Having endured the inquisition, presuming his ultimate acceptance, he would take a seat tainted and compromised by his performance before the Senate Judiciary Committee and by the trauma of realizing that he presented himself as a legal scholar but was treated and tested as a politician. Everyone else was running and he was made to run also. Alas, he was running on the wrong ticket.

It wasn't Biden who sent the most vulnerable nominee conceivable to the political piranhas of presidential politics. But the parallel is quite apparent. Both Biden and Bork were peculiarly vulnerable and the superlatively educated, politically advantaged could muster no restraint, no memory of the Golden Rule, nor ethical inhibitions of any kind. That is why most thoughtful individuals waste little sympathy on the periodic sad plights of politicians.

The chief problem with plagiarism concepts is that the attribution expectations traverse courtesy, intellectual honesty, ethics and law. The magnitude of the offense is often in the eye of the beholder. Some of Senator Biden's supporters will lament his failure to observe attribution courtesies, but will forgive his errors. Those who excoriated Ronald Reagan for frequently resorting to parables cannot be completely comfortable with a candidate who frequently resorts to paraphrasing. His opponents will remind the world that his offenses extended beyond courtesy into more substantial issues of comparative ethics.

The senator has a real dilemma and the media won't let him forget it. If he plagiarized "unconsciously," he is a Charley McCarthy directed by another's voice. It is not a symmetrical dilemma. The other side is worse. He <u>knew</u> he was using the words of others, understood the ethics involved, didn't care, and expected the deception to pass unnoticed. What kind of a president do you want? One who doesn't know what he is saying, where it came from or what it meant? Or a president who is intellectually dishonest? His campaign could not continue. He would have been portrayed as the candidate who runs off at the mouth with other people's words.

Oral political rhetoric is a poor place for serious consideration of plagiarism issues. It is a precise measure of our ethics, our notions of plagiarism, and our rationality, that the <u>New York Times</u> would lend dignity to such charges and that the media would so sedulously attend to appearances to the total exclusion of content and significance. And here, the prosecution must rest. After the Biden-Kinnock-Bork connection, all else is anticlimax.

Summary

Those with long memories will recall Governor Romney of Michigan, Senator Muskie from Maine, and others whose political careers suddenly terminated as did Senator Hart's and quite probably Senator Biden's. Thousands of people were of the firm belief that the individuals concerned were exactly what the nation needed. One wept openly over a private matter, another said he was "brain washed," another denied philandering, and a fourth admitted to plagiarism. We may now add copying syntax as another mode of fatal slip on the way to nomination and higher office. Character assassination of chosen candidates is comparatively common, tending toward the politically bilateral.

Was it plagiarism or charges of plagiarism that may have changed the nation's and the world's destiny? It makes no difference. The significance is that it has happened. The educated world allowed it to happen, caused it to happen. And the evidence is that it really didn't know what it was doing, and worse, from the evidence of its lack of diligence, didn't really care. That makes Senator Biden an irrational sacrifice on the altar of intellectual sloth, while at the same time, the educated community permitted him free license to abuse the public trust, and very likely allowed plagiarism charges to turn the course of U.S. legal history.

The Biden case is a painful and dreadfully pointed reminder of the state of ethics of the educated elite. It had no uneducated participants. The case was addressed only on the grounds of superficial propriety; no deeper ethical concerns intruded such as Biden's deeper motivations, the collapse of ethics in the face of ideology, the shallowness and fragility of ethics, and the strength and ruthlessness of ideology. Who would belive that Senator Biden's twin legal traumas played no role in the conduct of his judiciary chairmanship? The mesmerizing focus was on the superficial. The virtues and vices of Senator Biden and Judge Bork were irrelevant, their divergent ideologies, pretextual. The deeper contest was pure ad hominem. Like the convergence of matter and antimatter, energy was released and after the blinding flash nothing was actually learned. Two candidacies had self-destructed. The world was no wiser.

X

DEFENSES

Plagiarism charges are understandably demoralizing, particularly if the flagrant plagiarizer didn't expect to be apprehended on the way to publication. As for the charges directed to the putatively innocent or marginally questionable cases, the dismay is of an entirely different order. For the technically and literally innocent, the damage of charges may be construed as irreparable. The battle for academic survival may be avoided as having nothing to gain in a long struggle of outcome unforeseen. All of those charged with plagiarism should know what the real options are irrespective of the merit of those charges. Even academics must agree that whatever offenses are committed in whatever areas, those charged are entitled to the best defenses that can be devised. No apology is made for assisting the worst plagiarist in fashioning a defense of use to all of the rest of the alleged offenders. Further, there is no way to contrive a monograph on plagiarism without indirectly instructing in the fine arts of verbal deception.

The Psychology of Defense

There are several lines of defense against plagiarism charges. All or any one of which could be useful or critical depending on circumstances. The civil rights/equal protection of the laws line of defense creates a "second front" option, but like most second fronts, the option is confined to the latter stages of the conflict. Further, this line has to show unequal treatment and some degree of personal injury to professional welfare, loss of academic respect, integrity, employability, salary, promotion, tenure, or academic position attributable to the charges.

Full mobilization of all aspects of defense is the only prudent policy if the civil rights/equal protection defense is to succeed. The internal procedures precedent to court action are all germane to the external case construction and presentation. Which means mastery of all aspects of plagiarism as a technical matter and the pertinent applications of academic freedom and due process in the scholarly arena. The internal lines of defense are innocence on grounds of lack of credible evidence, lack of intent to deceive, and the presence of extenuating and mitigating circumstances.

Unfortunately for the charged party, the charge tends to carry the imputation that entitlement to academic freedom and due process has been vitiated by the nature of the offense, which itself may be construed as a violation of academic freedom. Or having abused academic freedom, it is unsuitable to claim it as a defense. It is, therefore, all the more essential to assert academic freedom and due process rights because the courts can construe such rights as waived by default. An added reason is to draw the institution into debate on such rights and create a "paper trail" of evidence that may subsequently demonstrate additional evidence of unequal treatment under institutional procedures and guidelines.

Given the nature of the charge and the disposition of the academic community, the charged party should not assume that there will be any significant support by either individuals or academic agencies. The person charged can instantly become a pariah. Amicable academic associations tend to be shallow and the degree is quickly tested in adversity. If support can be found from individuals and agencies, it ought to be used and can be extremely helpful if some are disposed to spend time and effort in research for the defense. No prior reliance on individuals or academic organizations is warranted until there is solid evidence of their support. The channels recruited can be reversed easily by the preponderant political power wielded by the institution and its officers and allies.

When to defend? One is tempted to say that all plagiarism charges are by some means defensible although the grounds may be more painful than the charges or even the proof of plagiarism. An example is intellectual incompetency of some species. For most cases, something like a cost-benefit analysis is required. Is there something material to be defended, like a tenured position, high academic reputation, promotion, salary, position? Is there a sufficient financial base to hire essential legal advice over periods of months or years and possibly the expense of court preparation and appearance? A rough estimate in going the full route--two to three years of gross salary. It is, however, a small fraction of an average, tenured, full career aggregate salary, assuming a successful defense.

Professional commitment and means should be considered quite apart from whether the individual charged has sufficient psychic resiliency to endure what may be, or what must in some circumstances become a protracted bitter contest with no assurance that the final outcome will favor the accused. Unfortunately, these issues and the decisions that must follow cannot be made on anything like a fully informed basis. It is true that resignation is always there as a last expedient and that fighting the charges at least (or worst) can buy time to more fully assess the actual merits of the case, and if weak, possibly afford cover for a "graceful retreat." A plausible defense combined with effective tactics might induce institutional second thoughts about pushing the charges to punitive levels. As noted earlier, the AAUP cautioned all parties in plagiarism cases of the potential embarrassment to both institutions and the accused in its Advisory Letter No. 15. For committed scholars, given a half a lifetime to the academy, who find the life a congenial and native environment, the decision to fight all but the most flagrant lapses of illicit copying should not be terribly difficult.

An Academic World of Evidence

The complete aggregate written exposition of any academic community means almost inevitably that there exists many articles, corporate writings, expository tracts, syllabi, charters and working papers, and, therefore, ample examples of copying, paraphrasing, borrowing of ideas, words, apt phrases, and larger and more serious extractions, deliberate and inadvertent of borrowing without source recognition. There will be examples that fit the symptoms and signs that comprise the traditional, casual notions of plagiarism. Finding them will be labor-intensive, but labor well spent. The closer the potential hurt of counter-charges approach the certain hurt of initial charges, the better the defense. In the game of plagiarism charges, the only safe individual is the one who has published nothing. It is a sorry comment that the prime defense against plagiarism is that "everybody's doing it, but I was singled out and here's the evidence." But this is also a stinging rebuke to the imprecision of its definition. It makes an enormous difference whether held to idealistic definitional standards or to de facto academic community standards of acknowledging usage of sources.

What are the probabilities of finding university publications of whatever order that offer examples of careless, even sloppy, citation modes? If the plaintiff wants to risk the patience of the court, the university could be dragged through "words, phrases, apt phrases, ideas, paraphrases," etc. not properly sourced. The chances are probably better than fifty-fifty that of faculties and administrative staffs running on the average about 1000 or more individuals that at least one, or a few, have offended the canons of plagiarism to the same degree as the individual charged. The odds are even fair for finding a worse offender. The best worst case, in legitimate defense, would be to find a second flagrant, unpunished plagiarizer, who would thereby get the first flagrant plagiarizer off the hook, on grounds that the university was not consistent in applying institutional rules.

A scholar defending against plagiarism charges will usually have the very great asset of scholarly competence that will need to be fully energized to the purposes of legal defense, not just accumulating and analyzing pertinent evidence for a counter suit, but laying out a prima facie case for review by civil rights agencies. Sometimes civil rights agencies will sue on behalf of the charged party or at minimum issue a "right to sue" letter that provides access to formal court attention. Because laws, procedures, policies, court decisions, and strategies are in perpetual flux, retaining legal counsel, while expensive, is always absolutely essential. For example, only recently the Supreme Court affirmed that Jews and Arabs could file civil rights cases under the 1866 Civil Rights Act that permitted what the Title VII statute did not, that is, damages. Hitherto, lower courts considered Arabs and Jews as Caucasians and white and, therefore, had no status before the court. Now that the highest court has extended civil rights umbrellas to all ethnic groups, perhaps it will identify the explicit non-ethnic group or groups entitled to no redress under the law. The Irish, for example? Swedes? One wonders what would be left: white males of mixed Anglo-Saxon ancestry?

The Civil Rights Defense

Civil rights litigations in which the central issue is plagiarism inevitably will find their way to court. As a legal strategy in plagiarism defenses it is a potentially devastating counter-attack to plagiarism charges. It is a "light at the end of the tunnel defense" because the usual position of the courts is that all internal forms of redress should be exhausted before formal legal petitions are made. It is the very protracted nature of internal proceedings, hearings, appeals, etc. that would induce the charged individual to give up the fight. That and the reality of the individual contesting against the institution that as a corporate body is immortal and has funds for legal purposes without limitations. But there is much to offset institutional advantages. All are entitled to equal protection of the laws. The route to the Federal Court is by evidence that whatever the charges were, whatever plagiarism was, all parties, i.e., the charging agency and the plaintiff were treated equally, consistently and explicitly free of bias.

The court really doesn't much care what universities and scholars consider to be plagiarism; that's their business. But if plagiarism, whatever it is, is used to punish an individual member, and that member is of a recognized minority, the university must approach the court, as the phrase goes, "with clean hands."

How untidy must those hands be to successfully serve the plaintiff? The court alone will decide. However, there are many hands to be inspected. All that is needed is a few pages of copying without proper attribution of source or sources by accusers who went unrebuked and unpunished. It also helps if those accused can claim minority status.

It will probably take all of the fun and lucre out of it, but in the U.S.A. there is no majority, only minorities of different sizes, races, ethnicities, values, behaviors, and persuasions. Some minorities currently enjoy preferred status that other minorities are denied. The minority white male, the minority most likely to be charged with plagiarism, is also entitled to equal protection under the laws. The brief below, at least in theory, would be equally supportable under civil rights or constitutional statutes.

A Civil Rights Brief

I. The defendant has taken the position that there is an institutional rule against plagiarism and that dismissal is an appropriate penalty for such an offense.

II. Whether dismissal occurred or was sought, the defendant's position is that the offense justified serious punishment. The evidence indicates that the plaintiff was denied salary increments and has been harassed and retaliated against as a consequence of the charges.

III. The defendant takes the position that the charges were "proved" although there is no evidence whatever of formal proof only sundry opinions as to what constituted proof by individuals who were parties to the proceedings against the plaintiff.

IV. The evidence accumulated in defense of the accused plaintiff demonstrates that:

A. There is no formal institutional rule for faculty against plagiarism.

B. That if such a rule existed de facto, the pattern of faculty peer compliance is a wide spread impunitive indifference to it.

C. In spite of categorical evidence of citation rule infractions, however labeled (plagiarism, expropriation, illicit borrowing, etc.), a minority member alone was punished, is being punished, and will continue to be punished by his employer unless granted legal relief.

V. The defendant has placed itself in the position that it must carry the burden that the rules of plagiarism, whatever they are, as applied, have not been, are not and will not be applied leniently to the non-minority and applied with special severity to a minority faculty member.

VI. The defendant must demonstrate that a legal justification exists for any different applications of the rules to minorities and non-minorities.

VII. The defendant must demonstrate that a legal justification exists for not invoking sanctions against non-minority faculty clearly and explicitly guilty of citation infractions both major and minor.

Defenses Ranked in Strength

I. Civil Rights: Academic due process and equal protection under the laws. Presumably now needs no further discussion.

II. Copying: No substantial copying occurred in either quantity or quality. The only weakness is defining the degrees and fending off sticklers to such definitions as the MLA's.

III. Intent: No positive evidence of intent to deceive. Inadvertent citation omissions plausible from the evidence. [See V below.]

IV. Addendum: The additions to the admittedly copied materials equal or exceed the value of the materials copied.

V. Acknowledgements: Sourcing present or proximate to copied materials in some form. Also reinforces the non-intentional defense.

VI. No Gain: No significant net gains from materials copied.

VII. Incompetency: The perfect Pyrrhic defense. Scholars and the educated are supposed to be both competent and to know better, as the Biden case clearly demonstrated.

VIII. Definition: Victim of the disparate definitions of plagiarism. Probably the weakest of the defenses, but it completes the circle back to using civil rights. Whatever the definition, under "equal treatment" provisions all are accountable.

But is this the way things ought to transpire in plagiarism? In the academy? Is this the best that we can do in what is, at core, an intellectual problem and not one necessarily of extreme complexity? Are the bilateral charges of plagiarism to be simply a brutal clash to determine the least offensive of contending offenders? It seems that until we can do better, equal treatment before the law remains the best and, in some instances, the only defense. Equitable treatment by intellectual analysis ought to precede the exercise of law. But exercise of intellect has thus far failed to provide a coherent definition of plagiarism. Must it also forever fail to find application in plagiarism charges? Will Lindey's "too much plagiarism crying" be exactly counterbalanced by too much crying of "you too?" There is something to be said for crude equity. It is better than no equity. Can we distill a refined equity fair to originator, paraphraser, and copier? If we can, we ought to.

XI

PROOF

Proof is an ideal that persistently retreats as we try to approach it. There are many kinds of operationally defined proofs applicable to diverse scholarly and technical areas. If any intellects have the capacity to weigh evidence and argument they ought to be found on college campuses in some reasonably representative numbers. The academy historically has tacitly assumed that proof of plagiarism is self-evident and that plagiarism consists of an aggregate of discrete singularities.

Among scholars of good will, it must be assumed that the null hypothesis is applicable to plagiarism with the same force it applies to other academic validations. It is equally invalid to affirm a false hypothesis as it is to reject a true one. The truth lives precariously balanced between the two classic forms of error. The opportunity for errors is always of more amplitude than the narrow precision required for truth. If this contention is accepted, then those of good will must accept the burdens of the formalities of proof which consist of formulating an hypothesis that inductively explains the alleged offensive behaviors. The null hypothesis stipulates that there are no behaviors present that meet the criteria. The burden of proof must be strong enough to reject that hypothesis.

A defensible definition must be in place to determine what behaviors are admissible as evidence. Both positive and negative criteria are reviewed for admissibility. Then each side should assume the role of devil's advocate for the opposition. The accused should build a best case for the chargers. The chargers should build a best case for the defense. If the grounds on either side are of equal strength, the case is not proved and the charges must be withdrawn or dropped. If the preponderance of evidence supports the charges, a measure of proof is present and the case may be pursued to some rational resolution.

How does one prove that plagiarism is provable? Unless it is always self-evident, assessment of alleged plagiarism must be based on some conceptual system. That system must, in turn, substitute specific criteria for the generalized accretions that time and intellectual inertia have permitted to burden the definition. Proof of plagiarism may indeed be in many instances more subtle than the theft of goods or money. But its proof should be no more difficult than fundamental issues raised in cases of libel and slander. Indeed, it ought to be more accessible to proof because the context involves not one document, but at least two, arising from two distinct sets of contexts, the originator and copier.

The formal entities of proof, evidence, testimony, argument, and probability are those absolutely requisite to any process to be dignified with the label of proof. Scholars especially are supposed to define terms carefully, weigh issues thoughtfully, analyze all pertinent evidence fairly, solicit objective external corroboration, avoid circular reasoning, isolate significant differences, avoid snap judgments, false assumptions, vague generalizations, and have the capacity and inclination to put ideas and definitions to the usual scholarly tests.

Further, scholars making charges and accusations must be fully appreciative of the rules of procedures governing whatever forms deliberations might take, and they need to know the AAUP rules of academic due process and the widely accepted documents that embody those rules. The documents are in the public domain. The general rules of equity and fair play from which they are derived are common knowledge. Proof of plagiarism cannot be made easy and in many cases it will be intrinsically difficult.

Readers can formulate their own standards of proof from the foregoing coverage of the six basic criteria, each of which is a variable that can take many values. Both trivial and gross copying should be isolated. Gross, explicitly deliberate, uncredited copying has only the defense of some form of incompetency. Between the trivial and the gross, proof must be by carefully defined criteria.

Valid, significant, original scholarship will always deserve protection from irrational copying. Sound work does not need an irrational defense nor should scholars in complicity and inequity avoid the intellectual obligation to make plagiarism a civilized model in both concept and process.

EPILOGUE

The view of this monograph is that plagiarism is not a malignant microcosm in the communicative macrocosm. The multiple continua of communication abound in gray areas of everyone's and no one's words. Much, perhaps most, of communication is purposely or inadvertently deceptive. Academies are supposed to penetrate and repudiate these practices. University presidents rarely write and read their own speeches. It is almost universally assumed that this little deceit is sanctioned by tradition.

Despite a legitimate measure of pessimism regarding academic ethics, this author is not inclined to believe that ethical indifference in the academy is by any means universal. Nor inclined to believe that the professoriate would not prefer to approach all of its problems with rigor and rationality if circumstances had not made even the simplest issues intractably complex. There is frustration everywhere, impatience all around, so that goodwill itself has turned hostile. What had seemed to be so obviously sensible and desirable must now be achieved by ideological collectivism and the simplistic mental gymnastics that inevitably follow.

The issue of plagiarism is as good a place as any to start the good fight to recapture the ethical high ground that the academy has traditionally claimed as its own. The ethics of academic indebtedness must be pursued with all the civility, rationality, and compassion that should characterize the academy at its best. Its understandings must be definitive even if its definitions are not. That is the direction to be sought.

Plagiarism is but one species of fraud in the academy or out, a verbal fraud aimed at its own kinds of illicit profit. In the academy it is falsification in the very arena of truth and for that reason the typical punishment has tended to be harsh. Because harsh and sometimes even brutal, the same commitment to truth that created concepts of plagiarism must now turn on itself to test its own validity and the ethical competencies of those who would invoke it.

<u>Plagiarism is an intentional verbal fraud committed by the psychologically competent that consists of copying significant and substantial uncredited written materials for unearned advantages with no significant enhancement of the materials copied.</u> This is plagiarism pure. It happens all to often. It is also all too often confused with plagiarism impure, mitigated, extenuated, marginal, hapless, ignorant, careless, etc. There are too many salients to plagiarism for a comprehensive definition. The underlined above is sufficiently rigorous to alert all readers with suspicions, warranted and otherwise, to essential discriminations that should and usually must precede judgments. In the light of these basics, the concerned

reader is then ready to address the context for the kind and degree of copying and proper courses of remediation if needed. Education and counseling will do for most. We can always go to court.

BIBLIOGRAPHY

Books

AAUP Policy Documents and Reports, 1977.

Black's Law Dictionary. West Publishing Company, 1951.

Bloom, Allan. Closing of the American Mind. Simon and Shuster, 1987.

Childress, William. Out of the Ozarks. Southern Illinois University Press, Carbondale, Illinois, 1987.

Cyclopedic Law Dictionary. Callaghan and Company, 1940.

Fowler, H. Ramsey. The Little Brown Handbook. Little, Brown and Company, 1980.

Hirsch, E. D., Jr. Cultural Literacy: What Every American Needs to Know. Houghton Mifflin, 1987.

Joughin, Louis, ed. Academic Freedom and Tenure: A Handbook of the AAUP. University of Wisconsin Press, 1969.

Lindey, Alexander. Plagiarism and Originality. Greenwood Press, 1952.

Martin, Harold C., and Ohmann, Richard M. The Logic and Rhetoric of Exposition. Holt, Rinehart and Winston, 1963.

The Oxford English Dictionary.

Paull, Harry M. Literary Ethics: A Study in the Growth of the Literary Conscience. London: T. Butterworth Limited, 1928.

St. Onge, Keith R. Creative Speech. Wadsworth Publishing Company, 1964.

Webster's New International Dictionary.

Webster's 3rd New International Dictionary.

White, Harold O. Plagiarism and Imitation During the English Renaissance. rpt. Octagon Books, 1965.

Periodicals

"A Charge of Plagiarism." The AAUP Bulletin, Letter No. 15 (Spring 1965).

Buckley, William. "Biden's Oratory Was Not Enough to Get By," St. Louis Post-Dispatch (September 9, 1987).

Cartwright, Phillip and Carol. "Software Development: Considerations for Promotions and Tenure," Academic Computing (Spring 1987).

"Notice." The Chronicle of Higher Education (June 10, 1987).

Greene, Bob. "Why a Person Steals Words," St. Louis Post-Dispatch (October 24, 1984).

Gunkel, Patrick. "An Idea Man Who Thinks in Lists," by David Stipp, The Wall Street Journal (June 1, 1987).

Hechinger, Fred M. "Has America Written Off Writing Ability?" The New York Times (1979).

Shapiro, Walter. "Whatever Happened to Ethics: What's Wrong," Time (May 25, 1987).

Shaw, Peter, "Plagiary," The American Scholar (Summer 1982).

Smith, Mike. "Brouhaha at Bo Jackson U.," St. Louis Post-Dispatch (August 21, 1987).

INDEX

Academic freedom, 36, 91
Academic Computing, 19
Alphabets, 13-14, 18-19
AAUP, 66, 67, 92-92, 100
American Scholar, 56, 104
Apt phrases, 2, 7, 27, 47, 69, 93
Aristotle, 16, 83
Artificial intelligence, 10
Autism, 6

Babbling, 12
Bennett, William, 37
Biden, Joseph, vii, 6, 63, 79-89
Black's Law Dictionary, 56
Bloom, Allan, 33, 35, 37
Bork, Robert, 80, 83-89
Boyer, Ernest, 37
Buckley, William, 6
Burger, Jeff, 40-41

Canonic knowledge, 25, 49
Cartwright, Phillip and Carol, 36
CNS, central nervous system, 14
Cheating, 39, 41
Childress, William, 1
Chimps, syntax, 14
Chronicle of Higher Education, 3, 4, 38, 75, 76
Churchill, 82
Civil rights, 36, 91, 93-97
Code, graphic, 12-16
  symbolic, 10
Conditioning, 18
Copyright, 28
Credibility, 26, 34, 35, 85
Cyclopedic Law Dictionary, 56

Daniel, Carter A., 3-4
Deception, 7, 22
Detection, 11, 19
Disinformation, 16, 33
Dogmas, 35
Doyle, Arthur Conan, 85
Due process, 64, 92
Dukakis, Michael, 87

Echolalia, 12
Education, costs, failures, 20-21
Einstein, 26
Eisenhower, 81, 84
Elitism, anti-elitism, 30, 38
EEOC, 83
Experts, 67

Factorials, 13, 47
Fleming, Alexander, 26
Formulation, 11-14, 18
Fowler, H. Ramsey, 103

Fraud, 51, 62, 64, 72, 74
Frost, Robert, 2

Galileo, 31
Germany, 22
Ghost writers, 8, 40, 42, 65
Graphic code, 18-19
Greene, Bob, 2-3
Guilt, 66, 67
Gunkel, Patrick, 27

Haley, Alex, 44
Hart, Gary, 81, 82, 88
Hechinger, Fred M., 21
Hirsch, E. D., Jr., 20
Hominid, 18
Hypotheses, null, 99
  research, 25

Ideas, the idea of, 4-5, 27, 47, 69
Ideology, 30, 31, 33, 35
Ideonomy, 27, 47
Idioglossia, 12
Image, 35, 38, 85
Infantolect, 15
Innate, non-innate, 14-15, 17
Inner language, 9, 12
Innocence, 22, 66, 67, 91
Intelligence, artificial, 10
  Biden's, 80, 82
  general, 40
IRS, 39

Jackson, Jesse, 83
Japan, 22
Jargon, 12
Jekyll and Hyde, 6
Joughlin, Louis, 103
Joyce, James, 6

Keats, 6
Kennedy(s), 81, 84, 85
Kinnock, Neil, 79-81
Kleptomania, 4-7

Lexical skills, 17, 22-23
Lincoln, 34, 82
Lindey, Alexander, x, 2, 4-5, 43, 44, 52-53, 59, 66, 97
Logic, 36-37
Los Angeles Times, 41

Malott, Dean, 6-7
Martin, Harold C., 55
McCarthy, Charley, 88
Memory, tonal, 6
  photographic, 6-7
Menjou, Adolphe, 6-7

Mental regimes, 5-6
Minorities, 35, 94-95
MLA, 52-55, 57, 63, 67, 76
Morale, faculty and student, 21, 39
Mozart, 6
Muskie, Ed, 88

NCAA, 40
Neologizing, 12
Neonates, 15
Newton, 28
New York Times, 21, 79, 80, 88
Nixon, Richard, 81, 85

Ochrymowycz, Leo, 3-4
Ohmann, Richard M., 55
Oral plagiarism, 9, 60, 65, 79
Originality, 8, 26-27, 43, 48, 50, 71
Orthographics, 19
Ostler, Scott, 41
OED, 56-57
Oxymoron, 34

Paragraphs, 47
Paraphrases, 22, 31, 42, 48, 81
Pathologies, of language, 16
Paull, Harry M., 103
Peer review, 28-29, 49
Personalities, multiple, 5-7
Phonemes, 11
Polemical research, 25, 30, 31
Pornography, 51
Pragmatics, language purposes, 16
Press, the, 82
Pretextual, 81, 88
Propositional, 47
Proust, 6
Ptolemy, 28
Public opinion polls, 20
Punctuation, 19
Punishment, 39, 42, 43

Reagan, Ronald W., 33, 81, 82, 88
Replication, 11-12, 19
Research, 29, 31
Rights, student, 36, 92
    minority, 93-97
Romney, George, 88
Roosevelt, Franklin, 81, 82

St. Louis Post-Dispatch, 1, 2, 6, 41, 79
Self-plagiarism, 4
Semantics, 47
Sentences, 47
Service, academic, 29, 31
Shakespeare, 2, 6
Shapiro, Walter, 33
Shaw, Peter, x, 4-5, 56
Signals, 11
Significance, 8, 26, 48, 50
Sin, 8, 37-38, 43
Smith, Mike, 41

Sophists, 18
Speech improvement, 17
Speech sounds, 11
Stipp, David, 27
Symbols, 11
Syntax, 13-15, 47
Systems, brain, 5

Teaching, 29, 31
Teaching Professor, 40-41
Tenure, 28, 35-57, 39, 45, 50, 64
Thatcher, Margaret, 79
Theft, ix, 17, 18, 22, 51, 61
Theories, 28
Time, 33
Tools, man and animals, 14, 16
Trivia, 20, 29
Truman, Harry, 84
Truth, 28, 37, 50

Unconscious plagiarism, 6
Uniqueness, 47
    research, 26-27
    sentences, 47
Universe, deceptive, 10
    models, 9-11
    variables, 10-11

Validity, 8, 26, 28-29, 48, 50
Verbal memory, 6-7
Vidal, Gore, 2
Voice, as carrier, 11
Vocabulary, 14

Wall Street Journal, 27
Watergate, 81
Webster's International Dictionary, 57
White, Harold O., 103
Writing skills, 18-21